7/12

THE ODES
OF HORACE

THE ODES
OF HORACE

A TRANSLATION BY

DAVID FERRY

FARRAR, STRAUS AND GIROUX

NEW YORK

Library of Congress Cataloging-in-Publication Data

Horace.
[Carmina. English. 1997]
The odes of Horace / a translation by David Ferry.
  p. cm.
ISBN 0-374-22425-0 (cloth : alk. paper)
  1. Horace—Translations into English.   2. Laudatory poetry, Latin—
Translations into English.   3. Verse satire, Latin—Translations
into English.   4. Rome—Poetry. I. Ferry, David.   II. Horace.
Carmen saeculare.   1997.   III. Title.
PA6395.F47   1997
874'.01—dc21   97-9483
                                                                        CIP

Some of these odes have previously appeared in: Agni, Arion,
Boston Phoenix, Boston Review, The Formalist, Gulf Coast,
Horace in English (ed. D. S. Carne-Ross and Kenneth Haynes;
Penguin Classics), Janus, Orion, Partisan Review, Pequod,
Persephone, Poetry Ireland, Raritan, Reading in an Age of
Theory (ed. Bridget Gellert Lyons; Rutgers University Press),
Slate, Southern Humanities Review, Strangers (David Ferry;
University of Chicago Press), Threepenny Review, and
TriQuarterly Review (a publication of Northwestern
University).

The Latin text used here is from Daniel Garrison's selection in
his Horace: Odes and Epodes, A New Annotated Latin
Edition (copyright © 1991 by Daniel H. Garrison), and is used
by permission of the University of Oklahoma Press.

This book is dedicated to D. S. Carne-Ross

and to the memory of Reuben A. Brower

Contents

Introduction

Horace (Quintus Horatius Flaccus) was born in Apulia, in the heel of the boot of Italy, in 65 B.C.E. His father was a well-to-do freedman who saw to it that his gifted son received a good education, first in Rome and then in Athens. While in Athens Horace joined the army of Brutus, two years after the assassination of Julius Caesar. He became a staff officer and fought, by his own account not very valiantly (Ode ii.7), at the battle of Philippi, where Octavian (later to be the emperor Augustus) and Mark Antony defeated Brutus. Apparently as a result, the property of Horace's family was confiscated. But Horace went to Rome and secured a position in the Treasury, and after some time, under the sponsorship of the poet Virgil, he was received into the literary circle around Octavian and his chief adviser, Maecenas. Maecenas, especially, became a close friend as well as Horace's patron. It was he who gave Horace his villa, the "Sabine farm," in the countryside a few miles from Rome, near Tibur (now called Tivoli).

In general the story of Horace's quiet life is the story of his writing. First there were the Satires, published in two books (late thirties B.C.E.), the first poems by which he received some recognition. In 29 he published his Epodes, in 23 the first three books of the Odes, and three years later the first book of his Epistles. In 17 B.C.E. he had the great honor of being asked by Augustus to write a ceremonial poem to be read at the Saecular Games Augustus organized to celebrate his own long reign. Three years after that he published his second book of Epistles, and a year later the fourth book of his Odes. It is not clear when the Epistle to Piso (the "Art of Poetry") was written.

Horace died in November, 8 B.C.E., shortly after (as he predicted in Ode ii.17) the death of Maecenas.

Donald Carne-Ross says of the Odes: "His great gift was to make the commonplace notable, even luminous, not to be discarded as part of the small change of existence."[1] "Commonplace" in two senses. The situations of many of the poems are pointedly ordinary: inviting a friend for a drink; proposing a party because of a friend's return from abroad, or to celebrate a birthday; wishing a friend a safe journey; advising somebody not to drink too much; praising a friend for his virtue, or his skill in poetry, or public affairs, or for his sexual success. Situations like these. Even the situations of the larger, more public poems are "commonplace" in the sense of being perfectly expectable and unsurprising: celebrating a victory or a ruler's homecoming; praising a ruler for his good rule; lamenting the vices and follies of the time;

addressing a god or goddess to praise the attributes appropriate to the particular divinity.

"Commonplace" in another sense too, not only in situation or occasion. When summed up or capsulized, the meanings of the poems are entirely expectable: "Stay in the middle, don't go too far out; remember that you are going to die, remember that you'll lose your good looks, that your love will alter, that you will grow old; don't be greedy, be content with what you have; power corrupts, riches corrupt, use them wisely; return to the ways of your virtuous ancestors; poetry immortalizes; poetry can do nothing against death." We greet such meanings, in this generalized form, without surprise.

The expectable has more than one function in art. It focuses our attention on performance; it provides recognizable configurations within which the unexpected can occur in interesting ways and in interesting kinds of tension with the familiar; it permits the artist to show how deep the familiar situation, theme, sentiment runs, how deeply it is founded on the truth, on what is commonplace because it is common to all of us. The expectable is, in Horace's hands, a kind of discipline, in something like the way the sonnet form is a kind of discipline, governing how we experience a particular sonnet, and how that sonnet varies and enlivens the form, or as meter is a discipline governing our experience of a particular line, and how the line becomes a vivid particular event.

The expectedness of situation or of theme frees us to focus on the particular performance of it in a given poem, and to experience that performance in relation to others. One of the great pleasures of the four books of Horace's odes is to see *how he will do it this time.* How will Horace telling Postumus (ii.14) that death is inevitable be different from Horace telling this to Dellius (ii.3), to Leuconoë (i.11), to Torquatus (iv.7), to Sestius (i.4)? The success of each is a challenge to the others, and part of the exhilaration for the reader is that Horace— "adroitest of artists," as Auden calls him[2]—meets the challenge every time. It's like watching a great diver being challenged by one perfect dive to perform yet another, of another kind and degree of difficulty, and another, and he does so. Ligurinus at his mirror, seeing the first signs of change in his beautiful face (iv.10), is being taught what's being taught to Lycia (iv.13), to Ibycus's wife (iii.15), to Lydia (i.25): that beauty goes, but in each case, in such a different way. Horace, for example, seems to have read Shakespeare's Sonnet 77 before he wrote the Ligurinus poem: "Thy glass will show thee how thy beauties wear, / Thy dial how thy precious minutes waste . . . The wrinkles which thy glass will truly show / Of mouthed graves will give thee memory . . ."

The cruel pity for Lycia's boozy singing, unwanted at the party, for her coming on to Cupid, who ignores her, transforms itself into Horace's heartbreaking, exalted reminiscence of his old ardor and of her beauty that deserved it. No moon shines, and the cold wind scatters dead leaves like Lydia, her beauty gone, her lovers no longer imploring her beneath her window. The lyre goes on being played at the revel, and there are wine and roses for Ibycus's daughter, but not for his self-deluding wife—*te lanae prope nobilem / tonsae Luceriam, non citharae decent / nec flos purpureus rosea / nec poti vetulam faece tenus cadi* ("for you, old girl, the famous // Knitting wool from Luceria is what's right; / What isn't right is the music of the lyre // In an atmosphere of dark red blooming roses, / And the wine jar emptied in the evening revel").

In one poem about poetry (i.6) it will be *Nos convivia, nos proelia virginum / sectis in iuvenes unguibus acrium / cantamus vacui, sive quid urimur, / non praeter solitum leves* ("It falls to me to make up easygoing // Songs about such battlefields as parties, / Epic encounters between young men and women. / Sometimes I write them because I've fallen in love. / Sometimes I write them just for the fun of it"); in another (iv.9), *Vixere fortes ante Agamemnona / multi; sed omnes illacrimabiles / urgentur ignotique longa / nocte, carent quia vate sacro* ("Heroes have lived before Agamemnon lived, / But all of them are lost somewhere in the night, / Unwept, unknown, unless they had a poet / To tell what was their story"); in another (iv.2), *Ego apis Matinae / more modoque // grata carpentis thyma per laborem / plurimum circa nemus uvidique / Tiburis ripas operosa parvus / carmina fingo* ("I // Am like the humble bee, painstakingly / Seeking to find the honey in the thyme / That grows in lowly fragrant groves and grows // Along the watery banks of Tivoli's stream; / My songs are made laboriously and slow"); in another (iii.30), *Exegi monumentum aere perennius / regalique situ pyramidum altius, / quod non imber edax, non Aquilo impotens / possit diruere aut innumerabilis / annorum series et fuga temporum* ("Today I have finished a work outlasting bronze / And the pyramids of ancient royal kings. / The North Wind raging cannot scatter it / Nor can the rain obliterate this work, / Nor can the years, nor can the ages passing"); and in another (i.31), *Frui paratis et valido mihi, / Latoë, dones ac, precor, integra / cum mente, nec turpem senectam / degere nec cithara carentem* ("Apollo grant that I be satisfied / With what I have as what I ought to have, // And that I live my old age out with honor, / In health of mind and body, doing my work").

Within the discipline of expectedness, not only from poem to poem but within a given poem, Horace is a dazzling shifter, almost, sometimes, a shape-shifter, as in ii.13, which begins hilariously cursing whatever man it was who planted the tree that fell, and almost fell on Horace, and almost killed him—*Illum et parentis crediderim sui / fregisse cervicem et penetralia / sparsisse nocturno cruore / hospitis* ("That man probably strangled his own father; / His hearth is probably stained with the blood of a houseguest / He murdered at midnight")—and then takes us on a breathtaking tonal journey that ends with the visionary scene of Hades, where Horace might have gone, where the shades listen in silence, spellbound to the shades of Sappho and Alcaeus, shoulder to shoulder thronging as they listen—*Utrumque sacro digna silentio / mirantur umbrae dicere; sed magis / pugnas et exactos tyrannos / densum umeris bibit aure vulgus.* This volatility of tone demonstrates itself over and over again, in countless ways, and in small instances as well as great. The little Ode i.8, for example, begins with Horace smilingly chiding Lydia for distracting Sybaris from his sport, and nothing in the tone of the quatrains that follow prepares us for the shift of scale to the sudden dark grandeur of the concluding lines: *Quid latet, ut marinae / filium dicunt Thetidis sub lacrimosa Troiae / funera, ne virilis / cultus in caedem et Lycias proriperet catervas?* ("Why does he seem to hide out, / The way that, they say, the son / Of sea-born Thetis, Achilles, // Hid out in the clothes of a woman, / Thinking the clothes of a woman / Would keep him out of the war, // Just as the war was starting / That brought the Trojans down / To their doom and all the tears?"). The shift in i.37, the Cleopatra ode, is famous, from the scornful opprobrium of *dum Capitolio / regina dementis ruinas, / funus et imperio parabat // contaminato cum grege turpium / morbo virorum, quidlibet impotens / sperare fortunaque dulci / ebria* (". . . that besotted queen, / With her vile gang of sick polluted creatures, // Crazed with hope and drunk with her past successes, / Was planning the death and destruction of the empire") to *saevis Liburnis scilicet invidens / privata deduci superbo / non humilis mulier triumpho* ("In truth—no abject woman she— she scorned / In triumph to be brought in galleys unqueened // Across the seas to Rome to be a show"). Such shifts in register are a demonstration of and a consequence of Horace's freedom.

To do his work within a framework of commonplaces, of expectable general meanings, implies a view of life. George Steiner, in *After Babel*, speaks of how in Horace "mastery of self, felicity, consist in a robust presentness . . . The note is that of domestic stoicism, of equability ensured by remembrance and disenchantment."[3] "Mastery of self," "robust presentness," "domestic," "equability," "insured," all suggest Horace's security in his knowledge of what is to be expected in his world, his place in that world, and in his self. A limitation of the expectable in a lesser artist might be complacency, both about himself, his own wisdom concerning the world he inhabits, and about that world, too, as if it, and its gods, were more predictable than they are, or as if what is predictable, expectable, was always going to be fortunate. Sometimes Horace pretends to that complacency and sometimes it's hard to distinguish, and not entirely to be distinguished, from his pleasure in himself and in the pleasure-giving world he inhabits, as in the marvelous little carefully self-arranged picture (Ode i.38) of himself, garlanded, drinking under his trees, attended by his garlanded slave. The poem confirms his pleasure in his pleasurable world; its "domestic . . . equability ensured by remembrance" of such pleasures in the past, and renewed in the present, tranquil pleasures made possible because Caesar has set the world in order and Maecenas has given Horace his Sabine villa. But there is "disenchantment" in it, too, in the unmistakable amusement at the picture of himself; this self-amusement distances him from himself and from his world. This distance is a form of freedom, and it makes room for other considerations, all of which have occurred in the book to which i.38 is the conclusion, and which occur in the other books of the odes as well. It is a freedom which knows (i.34) that the god may at any moment send his thunderbolt across the unclouded sky, and Atlas's pillar upholding the world may be shaken without notice. Horace's disenchantment, his freedom, knows about the capriciousness of the goddess Fortuna, who can dispossess even the most fortunate of their fortunes (i.35).

In Horace's view of things the unexpected is expected too, and the dire, and his stoical acceptance that this is so gives strength to a style which is unshakable in its clarity and force (Ode ii.10): *Saepius ventis agitatur ingens / pinus et celsae graviore casu / decidunt turres feriuntque summos / fulgura montis. / / Sperat infestis, metuit secundis / alteram sortem bene praeparatum / pectus* ("The tallest pine shakes most in a wind storm; / The loftiest tower falls down with the loudest crash; / The lightning bolt heads straight for the mountain top. / Always expect reversals: be hopeful in trouble, / Be worried when things go well. That's how it is / For the man whose heart is ready for anything"). The sentiment is familiar, but the authority with which it is said runs deep because so deeply founded on the truth, on what is commonplace because common to all.

Visendus ater flumine languido
Cocytos errans et Danaï genus
infame damnatusque longi
Sisyphus Aeolides laboris.

Linquenda tellus et domus et placens
uxor, neque harum quas colis arborum
*   te praeter invisas cupressos*
*   ulla brevem dominum sequetur.*

Absumet heres Caecuba dignior
servata centum clavibus et mero
*   tinguet pavimentum superbo*
*   pontificum potiore cenis.*

Each one of us shall come to see the black
River Cocytos wandering through the region
Where Danaus' wicked daughters endlessly suffer
And Sisyphus for ever labors on.

Each one of us must leave the earth he loves
And leave his home and leave his tender wife,
And leave the trees he planted and took good care of.
Only the cypress grows along those banks.

Your heir will drink the choice Caecuban wine
You did not know that you were saving for him
When you locked it up securely in your cellar.
The wine he spills is priceless, it doesn't matter.

                                                (ii.14)

NOTE ON THE TRANSLATIONS

In these translations I have tried, generally speaking, to be as faithful
as I could be to Horace's poems. English of course is not Latin and I
am most certainly not Horace. Every act of translation is an act of
interpretation, and every choice of English word or phrase, every
placement of those words or phrases in sentences—made in obedience
to the laws and habits of English, not Latin, grammar, syntax, and
idioms—and every metrical decision—made in obedience to English,
not Latin, metrical laws and habits—reinforce the differences between
the interpretation and the original. This is true however earnestly the
interpretation aims to represent the sense of Horace's odes, the effects
and implications of his figures of speech, the controlled volatility of his
tones of voice. As translations of these Odes go, it is my hope that this

one, granting these differences between English and Latin, is reasonably close.

There are a few places where I have, however, deliberately gone pretty far away from the Latin poem, by substitution or by omission, for example, in my rendering of the conclusion of the famous "Soracte ode" (i.9) or of the ode about Maecenas's wife (ii.12). In both these cases I thought that stricter faithfulness would have made it more difficult to produce a viable English poem. Several times I have provided an anachronistically modern equivalent for something ancient and unfamiliar, for example, "Ouija board" for "Babylonian numbers." Occasionally I have taken advantage of scholarly disagreements, as in my reading of the Archytas ode (i.28). But there are not many such places.

Sometimes my translation reflects the way I have heard the rhythms of the Latin of this or that line or passage, and sometimes a whole poem will be set in a meter which is a kind of allusion to a Latin meter (for example, the faux-Sapphic meter of my translation of the "Carmen Saeculare"). But I have not tried systematically to reproduce or imitate the Latin meters of these odes, since English meters are so different. I have tried to represent in a general way Horace's formal variety by working in a variety (but by no means a wide variety) of combinations of metrical lines, mainly pentameter lines although occasionally trimeter or hexameter, but the basic foot always remains iambic, with rather frequent anapestic, and with some trochaic, substitutions.

In some cases the Glossary and the Notes give indications for stressing proper names.

D.F.

BOOK ONE

Maecenas atavis edite regibus,
o et praesidium et dulce decus meum,
sunt quos curriculo pulverem Olympicum
collegisse iuvat metaque fervidis
evitata rotis palmaque nobilis
terrarum dominos evehit ad deos;
hunc, si mobilium turba Quiritium
certat tergeminis tollere honoribus,
illum, si proprio condidit horreo
quicquid de Libycis verritur areis.
Gaudentem patrios findere sarculo
agros Attalicis condicionibus
numquam dimoveas, ut trabe Cypria
Myrtoum pavidus nauta secet mare.
Luctantem Icariis fluctibus Africum
mercator metuens otium et oppidi
laudat rura sui; mox reficit rates
quassas, indocilis pauperiem pati.
Est qui nec veteris pocula Massici
nec partem solido demere de die
spernit, nunc viridi membra sub arbuto
stratus, nunc ad aquae lene caput sacrae.
Multos castra iuvant et lituo tubae
permixtus sonitus bellaque matribus
detestata. Manet sub Iove frigido
venator tenerae coniugis immemor,
seu visa est catulis cerva fidelibus,
seu rupit teretes Marsus aper plagas.

Maecenas, you, descended from many kings,
O you who are my stay and my delight,
There is the man whose glory it is to be
So famous even the gods have heard the story

Of how his chariot raised Olympic dust,
The dazzling wheel making the smoking turn;
And there is he whose bliss it is to be carried
Up to the honors of office on the shifting

Shoulders of the crowd; and he whose pride
Is that his barns hold everything that can
Be gathered from the Libyan fields of grain.
And there's the man who with his little hoe

Breaks the hard soil of his poor father's farm,
But all the money there is could never persuade him
To venture out on the sea, a quaking sailor.
And the fearful trader in his wallowing vessel

As the storm comes on longs for his native village
And longs for the quiet fields surrounding it—
And then of course next year refits his ship,
Unable to forgo the profit of it.

And there's the man who likes his cup of wine,
Taking his ease in the busiest time of the day,
Under the shady boughs of the green arbutus
Or near the secret source of some murmuring brook.

There are those who love encampments, and love the confused
Music of trumpet and clarion sounding together
And are in love with the wars their mothers hate.
And all night long, out in the bitter cold,

If his faithful dogs have startled up a deer
Or if a wild boar has broken through the snare,
The hunter waits, forgetful of his bride;
All night the bride at home waits for the hunter.

Me doctarum hederae praemia frontium
dis miscent superis, me gelidum nemus
Nympharumque leves cum Satyris chori
secernunt populo, si neque tibias
Euterpe cohibet nec Polyhymnia
Lesboum refugit tendere barbiton.
Quodsi me lyricis vatibus inseres,
sublimi feriam sidera vertice.

What links *me* to the gods is that I study
To wear the ivy wreath that poets wear.
The cool sequestered grove in which I play
For nymphs and satyrs dancing to my music

Is where I am set apart from other men—
Unless the muse Euterpe takes back the flute
Or Polyhymnia untunes the lyre.
But if *you* say I am truly among the poets,

Then my exalted head will knock against the stars.

Iam satis terris nivis atque dirae
grandinis misit pater et rubente
dextera sacras iaculatus arces
    terruit urbem,

terruit gentis, grave ne rediret
saeculum Pyrrhae nova monstra questae,
omne cum Proteus pecus egit altos
    visere montes,

piscium et summa genus haesit ulmo,
nota quae sedes fuerat columbis,
et superiecto pavidae natarunt
    aequore dammae.

Vidimus flavum Tiberim, retortis
litore Etrusco violenter undis,
ire deiectum monumenta regis
    templaque Vestae,

Iliae dum se nimium querenti
iactat ultorem, vagus et sinistra
labitur ripa, Iove non probante, ux-
    orius amnis.

Audiet civis acuisse ferrum,
quo graves Persae melius perirent,
audiet pugnas vitio parentum
    rara iuventus.

Quem vocet divum populus ruentis
imperi rebus? Prece qua fatigent
virgines sanctae minus audientem
    carmina Vestam?

Cui dabit partis scelus expiandi
Iuppiter? Tandem venias, precamur,
nube candentis umeros amictus,
    augur Apollo;

Jupiter the Father has brought down
A storm of snow and hail upon the city.
Striking the Capitol with his hand of fire,
He has terrified the city and the people.

Maybe the age of Pyrrha has come back,
The dreadful time when Proteus drove his herd
Up out of the sea and up the mountainsides
And there were living creatures from the sea

Entangled in the highest elm-tree branches
Where doves had cooed and nested, and in the water
Fear-maddened deer and other land-beasts struggled.
We witnessed how the Tiber, wild, thrown back

From against the Tuscan shore, ran loose and up
(Too ardent avenger of his beloved Ilia)
Over the other shore, washing against
The Regia and the temple of Vesta themselves.

The decimated people, our descendants,
Diminished by the vices of their fathers,
Will hear someday how citizens whetted their swords,
Which might have been better used against the Parthians,

Upon each other's bodies. What god can the people
Pray to, to save the state? What prayer can the Vestal
Virgins pray, if Vesta will not listen?
What god will come to expiate our crimes?

Augur Apollo, descend, your radiant shoulders
Clad in radiant cloud; or smiling Venus,
Laughter and love attending you, come down;
Unless you have forgotten us your children,

Come to our aid, O Mars, at last perhaps
Fed up with the game of war played on too long,
The battle cry, the glitter and gleam of arms,
Bloodhungry face confronting bloodhungry face;

sive tu mavis, Erycina ridens,
quam Iocus circum volat et Cupido;
sive neglectum genus et nepotes
    respicis, auctor,

heu nimis longo satiate ludo,
quem iuvat clamor galeaeque leves
acer et Marsi peditis cruentum
    vultus in hostem;

sive mutata iuvenem figura
ales in terris imitaris almae
filius Maiae, patiens vocari
    Caesaris ultor:

serus in caelum redeas, diuque
laetus intersis populo Quirini,
neve te nostris vitiis iniquum
    ocior aura

tollat; hic magnos potius triumphos,
hic ames dici pater atque princeps,
neu sinas Medos equitare inultos,
    te duce, Caesar.

Or wingèd Mercury, son of beneficent Maia,
Descend to help us, disguising yourself perhaps
In the form of that young man prepared to avenge
The murder of his kinsman Julius Caesar.

If this be so, may it be so for long;
Let it not come about that you, too soon,
Offended by Roman crimes, are carried back
Up to the heavens from which you came to help us;

May Caesar be content to dwell among
The children who descend from Romulus,
Enjoying the name of Father and of Prince;
Because of him no Parthians raid unpunished.

i.3

Sic te diva potens Cypri,
  sic fratres Helenae, lucida sidera,
ventorumque regat pater
  obstrictis aliis praeter Iäpyga,

navis, quae tibi creditum
  debes Vergilium; finibus Atticis
reddas incolumem, precor,
  et serves animae dimidium meae.

Illi robur et aes triplex
  circa pectus erat, qui fragilem truci
commisit pelago ratem
  primus, nec timuit praecipitem Africum

decertantem Aquilonibus
  nec tristis Hyadas nec rabiem Noti,
quo non arbiter Hadriae
  maior, tollere seu ponere vult freta.

Quem mortis timuit gradum
  qui siccis oculis monstra natantia,
qui vidit mare turbidum et
  infamis scopulos, Acroceraunia?

Nequiquam deus abscidit
  prudens Oceano dissociabili
terras, si tamen impiae
  non tangenda rates transiliunt vada.

Audax omnia perpeti
  gens humana ruit per vetitum nefas.
Audax Iapeti genus
  ignem fraude mala gentibus intulit.

Post ignem aetheria domo
  subductum macies et nova febrium
terris incubuit cohors,
  semotique prius tarda necessitas

May Venus goddess of Cyprus and may the brothers
Castor and Pollux, the shining stars, the calmers,
Guard you, O ship, and be the light of guidance;
May the father of the winds restrain all winds
Except the gentle one that favors this journey.
Bring Virgil, your charge, the other half of my heart,
Safely to the place where he is going.

The breast of the man who was the first to dare
To go out in a little boat upon the waters
Must have been made of oak and triple bronze,
Fearing neither the sudden African squall
Contending with the North Wind, nor the storms
The Hyades threaten, nor what the South Wind, Notus,
Who rules the Adriatic, is capable of.

What way of dying could that man have feared
Who dared to be the first to look upon
The swimming monsters, the turbulent waters and
The dreadful cliffs of Acroceraunia?
The purpose of the god who separated
One land from another land was thwarted
If impious men could nevertheless set out

To cross the waters forbidden to them to cross.
Audacious at trying out everything, men rush
Headlong into the things that have been forbidden.
Guileful Prometheus audaciously by fraud
Brought fire down to the human race and thus
Brought fever down upon us and disease,
And death that once was slow to come came sooner.

Audacious Daedalus, wearing forbidden wings,
Tried out the empty air. And Hercules
Went down to the Underworld, broke in and entered.
No hill's too steep for men to try to climb;

leti corripuit gradum.
  Expertus vacuum Daedalus aëra
pinnis non homini datis;
  perrupit Acheronta Herculeus labor.

Nil mortalibus ardui est;
  caelum ipsum petimus stultitia, neque
per nostrum patimur scelus
  iracunda Iovem ponere fulmina.

Men even try out getting up to Heaven.
Is it any wonder, then, that Jupiter rages,
Hurling down lightning, shaking the sky with thunder?

Solvitur acris hiems grata vice veris et Favoni,
  trahuntque siccas machinae carinas,
ac neque iam stabulis gaudet pecus aut arator igni,
  nec prata canis albicant pruinis.

Iam Cytherea choros ducit Venus imminente luna,
  iunctaeque Nymphis Gratiae decentes
alterno terram quatiunt pede, dum gravis Cyclopum
  Vulcanus ardens visit officinas.

Nunc decet aut viridi nitidum caput impedire myrto
  aut flore, terrae quem ferunt solutae;
nunc et in umbrosis Fauno decet immolare lucis,
  seu poscat agna sive malit haedo.

Pallida Mors aequo pulsat pede pauperum tabernas
  regumque turris. O beate Sesti,
vitae summa brevis spem nos vetat incohare longam.
  Iam te premet nox fabulaeque Manes

et domus exilis Plutonia; quo simul mearis,
  nec regna vini sortiere talis,
nec tenerum Lycidan mirabere, quo calet iuventus
  nunc omnis et mox virgines tepebunt.

Now the hard winter is breaking up with the welcome coming
  Of spring and the spring winds; some fishermen,
Under a sky that looks changed, are hauling their caulked boats
  Down to the water; in the winter stables the cattle
Are restless; so is the farmer sitting in front of his fire;
  They want to be out of doors in field or pasture;
The frost is gone from the meadow grass in the early mornings.
  Maybe, somewhere, the Nymphs and Graces are dancing,
Under the moon the goddess Venus and her dancers;
  Somewhere far in the depth of a cloudless sky
Vulcan is getting ready the storms of the coming summer.
  Now is the time to garland your shining hair
With myrtle or with the flowers the free-giving earth has given;
  Now is the right time to offer the kid or lamb
In sacrifice to Faunus in the firelit shadowy grove.

Revenant white-faced Death is walking not knowing whether
  He's going to knock at a rich man's door or a poor man's.
O good-looking fortunate Sestius, don't put your hope in the future;
  The night is falling; the shades are gathering around;
The walls of Pluto's shadowy house are closing you in.
  There who will be lord of the feast? What will it matter,
What will it matter there, whether you fell in love with Lycidas,
  This or that girl with him, or he with her?

Quis multa gracilis te puer in rosa
perfusus liquidis urget odoribus
   grato, Pyrrha, sub antro?
     Cui flavam religas comam,

simplex munditiis? Heu quotiens fidem
mutatosque deos flebit et aspera
   nigris aequora ventis
     emirabitur insolens

qui nunc te fruitur credulus aurea,
qui semper vacuam, semper amabilem
   sperat, nescius aurae
     fallacis. Miseri, quibus

intemptata nites. Me tabula sacer
votiva paries indicat uvida
   suspendisse potenti
     vestimenta maris deo.

What perfumed debonair youth is it, among
  The blossoming roses, urging himself upon you
In the summer grotto? For whom have you arranged
  Your shining hair so elegantly and simply?

How often will he weep because of betrayal,
  And weep because of the fickleness of the gods,
Wondering at the way the darkening wind
  Suddenly disturbs the calm waters.

Now he delights in thinking how lovely you are,
  Vacant of storm as the fragrant air in the garden—
Not knowing at all how quickly the wind can change.
  Hapless are they enamored of that beauty

Which is untested yet. And as for me?
  The votive tablet on the temple wall
Is witness that in tribute to the god
  I have hung up my sea-soaked garment there.

i.6

Scriberis Vario fortis et hostium
victor, Maeonii carminis alite,
quam rem cumque ferox navibus aut equis
    miles te duce gesserit.

Nos, Agrippa, neque haec dicere nec gravem
Pelidae stomachum cedere nescii
nec cursus duplicis per mare Ulixeï
    nec saevam Pelopis domum

conamur, tenues grandia, dum pudor
imbellisque lyrae Musa potens vetat
laudes egregii Caesaris et tuas
    culpa deterere ingeni.

Quis Martem tunica tectum adamantina
digne scripserit aut pulvere Troico
nigrum Merionen aut ope Palladis
    Tydiden superis parem?

Nos convivia, nos proelia virginum
sectis in iuvenes unguibus acrium
cantamus vacui, sive quid urimur,
    non praeter solitum leves.

i.6 / *To Agrippa*

It takes a poet such as Varius,
Capable of Homeric flight and range,
To praise your deeds of courage and the events
Of victory whether by ship or cavalry.

I don't pretend to sing about such things
As the stubborn peevish anger of Achilles
Or duplicitous Ulysses' wanderings or
The ferocious House of Atreus. Not for me.

Self-knowledge and the Muse of peaceful things
Prohibit me from dimming with my verses
Your glory and the glory of great Caesar.
Who is it who is worthy to write the story

Of Mars in his adamantine armor, or
Of Meriones covered with Trojan dust
Or Diomedes in battle against two gods?
It falls to me to make up easygoing

Songs about such battlefields as parties,
Epic encounters between young men and women.
Sometimes I write them because I've fallen in love.
Sometimes I write them just for the fun of it.

Laudabunt alii claram Rhodon aut Mytilenen
   aut Epheson bimarisve Corinthi
moenia vel Baccho Thebas vel Apolline Delphos
   insignis aut Thessala Tempe.

Sunt quibus unum opus est intactae Palladis urbem
   carmine perpetuo celebrare et
undique decerptam fronti praeponere olivam;
   plurimus in Iunonis honorem

aptum dicet equis Argos ditisque Mycenas:
   me nec tam patiens Lacedaemon
nec tam Larisae percussit campus opimae,
   quam domus Albuneae resonantis

et praeceps Anio ac Tiburni lucus et uda
   mobilibus pomaria rivis.
Albus ut obscuro deterget nubila caelo
   saepe Notus neque parturit imbris

perpetuos, sic tu sapiens finire memento
   tristitiam vitaeque labores
molli, Plance, mero, seu te fulgentia signis
   castra tenent seu densa tenebit

Tiburis umbra tui. Teucer Salamina patremque
   cum fugeret, tamen uda Lyaeo
tempora populea fertur vinxisse corona,
   sic tristis affatus amicos:

Others may give their praise to famous Rhodes,
Or Mitylene, or Ephesus, or else
To Corinth from whose walls two seas are seen,
Or Bacchus' birthplace, Thebes, or to the Vale

Of Tempe, or Apollo's sacred Delphi;
Some wearing the laurel wreath whose leaves are plucked
From the laurel wreaths that earlier praisers wore,
Unwearied as their only song sing praise

In honor of the city of Pallas Athena;
And many in praise of Juno retell the story
Of Argos and its horses, and rich Mycenae.
As far as I'm concerned, not even hardy

Sparta or the grainfields of Larisa
Take hold of my imagination as
The echoing Albunean grotto does,
Or the waterfall of the Anio or the sacred

Forest of Tibur and its quiet orchards,
Watered by the river passing by.
Just as Notus the South Wind isn't always
What he often is, the bringer-on of storms,

But sometimes clears the clouds away instead,
So, Plancus, be wise enough, wherever you are,
Whether you're camped on the battlefield, among
The shining weapons and the battle standards,

Or else at home in your shady groves at Tibur,
To put aside for a while, with the help of wine,
The cares and the anxieties of life.
The story goes that Teucer, when he fled

From Salamis and from his father's wrath,
Florid with wine, garlanded his head
And said these words to his troubled followers:
"Dear friends, companions, let us go where Fortune,

"Quo nos cumque feret melior fortuna parente,
  ibimus, o socii comitesque.
Nil desperandum Teucro duce et auspice Teucro;
  certus enim promisit Apollo

ambiguam tellure nova Salamina futuram.
  O fortes peioraque passi
mecum saepe viri, nunc vino pellite curas;
  cras ingens iterabimus aequor."

Kinder than my father, wants us to go.
Have confidence in Teucer and the omens.
Apollo never errs and he has promised
Another Salamis somewhere in the world.

O my brave fellows who have gone through worse
Than this with me, now with the help of wine
Let's put aside our troubles for a while.
Tomorrow we set out on the vast ocean."

i.8

Lydia, dic per omnis
  hoc deos vere, Sybarin cur properes amando
perdere, cur apricum
  oderit campum, patiens pulveris atque solis,

cur neque militaris
  inter aequalis equitet, Gallica nec lupatis
temperet ora frenis.
  Cur timet flavum Tiberim tangere? Cur olivum

sanguine viperino
  cautius vitat neque iam livida gestat armis
bracchia, saepe disco,
  saepe trans finem iaculo nobilis expedito?

Quid latet, ut marinae
  filium dicunt Thetidis sub lacrimosa Troiae
funera, ne virilis
  cultus in caedem et Lycias proriperet catervas?

For God's sake, Lydia, tell me,
  Why are you so determined
    To ruin Sybaris

With love, the way you do?
  Why has he taken such
    A dislike to the sunny Campus,

He who used to put up with
  The dust and heat of the games,
    Liking it fine. Why doesn't

He who knew how to manage
  The bit and the bridle with such
    Elegance, why doesn't

He ride anymore these days?
  Why does he act as if
    He's afraid to go into the Tiber?

Why does he act as if
  The olive oil he used
    To oil his body with

Before the wrestling match
  Is the blood of a poisonous snake?
    He used to be famous for throwing

The discus and javelin too,
  Far out beyond the farthest
    Throw of his nearest rival.

Why do his arms not show
  The bruises that are the signs
    Of practicing with these weapons?

Why does he seem to hide out,
  The way that, they say, the son
    Of sea-born Thetis, Achilles,

Hid out in the clothes of a woman,
  Thinking the clothes of a woman
    Would keep him out of the war,

Just as the war was starting
  That brought the Trojans down
    To their doom and all the tears?

Vides ut alta stet nive candidum
Soracte, nec iam sustineant onus
    silvae laborantes, geluque
        flumina constiterint acuto.

Dissolve frigus ligna super foco
large reponens atque benignius
    deprome quadrimum Sabina,
        o Thaliarche, merum diota.

Permitte divis cetera, qui simul
stravere ventos aequore fervido
    deproeliantis, nec cupressi
        nec veteres agitantur orni.

Quid sit futurum cras fuge quaerere, et
quem Fors dierum cumque dabit lucro
    appone, nec dulcis amores
        sperne puer neque tu choreas,

donec virenti canities abest
morosa. Nunc et campus et areae
    lenesque sub noctem susurri
        composita repetantur hora,

nunc et latentis proditor intimo
gratus puellae risus ab angulo
    pignusque dereptum lacertis
        aut digito male pertinaci.

i.9 / *To Thaliarchus*

See Mount Soracte shining in the snow.
See how the laboring overladen trees
Can scarcely bear their burdens any longer.

See how the streams are frozen in the cold.
Bring in the wood and light the fire and open
The fourth-year vintage wine in the Sabine jars.

O Thaliarchus, as for everything else,
Forget tomorrow. Leave it up to the gods.
Once the gods have decided, the winds at sea

Will quiet down, and the sea will quiet down,
And these cypresses and old ash trees will shake
In the storm no longer. Take everything as it comes.

Put down in your books as profit every new day
That Fortune allows you to have. While you're still young,
And while morose old age is far away,

There's love, there are parties, there's dancing and there's music,
There are young people out in the city squares together
As evening comes on, there are whispers of lovers, there's laughter.

Mercuri, facunde nepos Atlantis,
qui feros cultus hominum recentum
voce formasti catus et decorae
    more palaestrae,

te canam, magni Iovis et deorum
nuntium curvaeque lyrae parentem,
callidum quicquid placuit iocoso
    condere furto.

Te, boves olim nisi redidisses
per dolum amotas, puerum minaci
voce dum terret, viduus pharetra
    risit Apollo.

Quin et Atridas duce te superbos
Ilio dives Priamus relicto
Thessalosque ignis et iniqua Troiae
    castra fefellit.

Tu pias laetis animas reponis
sedibus virgaque levem coerces
aurea turbam, superis deorum
    gratus et imis.

O fluent Mercury, grandchild of Atlas, you
Who gave the means of order to the ways
Of early men by giving speech to them
And laying down the rules of the wrestling-floor,

Where grace is learned in the intricacy of play,
It is your praise I sing, O messenger
Of Jupiter and of the other gods,
Clever deviser of the curvèd lyre,

Hider-away of anything you please
It pleases you to hide. The day you were born
You stole Apollo's cattle away from him;
Apollo had to laugh when he found out

That while he stormed and threatened you'd stolen away
His quiver and arrows too. You stole away
Priam of Troy from Troy, bearing possessions,
Guiding him past the light of Thessalian watchfires,

Past the enemy camp of the arrogant Greeks.
You guide the pious dead to their place of bliss;
With your golden wand you shepherd the ghostly flock.
You please both the gods above and those below.

Tu ne quaesieris—scire nefas—quem mihi, quem tibi
finem di dederint, Leuconoë, nec Babylonios
temptaris numeros. Ut melius quicquid erit pati,
seu pluris hiemes, seu tribuit Iuppiter ultimam,
quae nunc oppositis debilitat pumicibus mare
Tyrrhenum. Sapias, vina liques, et spatio brevi
spem longam reseces. Dum loquimur, fugerit invida
aetas: carpe diem, quam minimum credula postero.

Don't be too eager to ask
  What the gods have in mind for us,
What will become of you,
  What will become of me,
What you can read in the cards,
  Or spell out on the Ouija board.
It's better not to know.
  Either Jupiter says
This coming winter is not
  After all going to be
The last winter you have,
  Or else Jupiter says
This winter that's coming soon,
  Eating away the cliffs
Along the Tyrrhenian Sea,
  Is going to be the final
Winter of all. Be mindful.
  Take good care of your household.
The time we have is short.
  Cut short your hopes for longer.
Now as I say these words,
  Time has already fled
Backwards away—
  Leuconoë—
    Hold on to the day.

Quem virum aut heroa lyra vel acri
tibia sumis celebrare, Clio?
Quem deum? Cuius recinet iocosa
    nomen imago

aut in umbrosis Heliconis oris
aut super Pindo gelidove in Haemo,
unde vocalem temere insecutae
    Orphea silvae,

arte materna rapidos morantem
fluminum lapsus celerisque ventos,
blandum et auritas fidibus canoris
    ducere quercus?

Quid prius dicam solitis parentis
laudibus, qui res hominum ac deorum,
qui mare ac terras variisque mundum
    temperat horis?

Unde nil maius generatur ipso,
nec viget quicquam simile aut secundum;
proximos illi tamen occupavit
    Pallas honores,

proeliis audax; neque te silebo,
Liber, et saevis inimica virgo
beluis, nec te, metuende certa
    Phoebe sagitta.

Dicam et Alciden puerosque Ledae,
hunc equis, illum superare pugnis
nobilem; quorum simul alba nautis
    stella refulsit,

defluit saxis agitatus umor,
concidunt venti fugiuntque nubes,
et minax, quod sic voluere, ponto
    unda recumbit.

i.12 / *To Clio*

Whom do you choose to celebrate, O Clio?
Is it a man? or hero half-divine?

Is it a god? Whose name will Echo echo
Playfully? Upon what mountainside?

From Helicon's shadows or from the height of Pindus?
Or is it cold Mount Haemus whence the trees

In rapt confusion followed after the voice
Of Orpheus singing as his mother taught him—

That voice to hear whose song the rushing streams
Fell silent and the winds' commotion stilled?

Whom shall I praise before the ordained praise
Of the father god, of Jupiter himself,

Who sets in order the things of men and gods,
Of seas, and lands, and all the changing hours?

Of those he has begotten there is none
Greater than he nor is there any god

Whose glory comes near his glory—yet there's one
Whose glory comes nearest his of all the gods,

Pallas Athena, mighty in battle—and then
There's Bacchus, and the virgin goddess who

Chastises all the beasts, and there's Apollo,
Whose never-missing arrow terrifies;

Then Hercules, and the twin sons of Leda,
The horseman and the boxer—because of them,

When in the nighttime sky their constellation
Makes itself known, the turbulent waters crashing

Romulum post hos prius an quietum
Pompili regnum memorem an superbos
Tarquini fasces, dubito, an Catonis
    nobile letum.

Regulum et Scauros animaeque magnae
prodigum Paulum superante Poeno
gratus insigni referam camena
    Fabriciumque.

Hunc et incomptis Curium capillis
utilem bello tulit et Camillum
saeva paupertas et avitus apto
    cum lare fundus.

Crescit occulto velut arbor aevo
fama Marcelli; micat inter omnis
Iulium sidus, velut inter ignis
    luna minores.

Gentis humanae pater atque custos,
orte Saturno, tibi cura magni
Caesaris fatis data: tu secundo
    Caesare regnes.

Ille seu Parthos Latio imminentis
egerit iusto domitos triumpho,
sive subiectos Orientis orae
    Seras et Indos,

Against the rocky shore subside, and the wind
Blows gently, if at all. Next come the Romans:

I don't know which of them to celebrate first.
Romulus, perhaps, who was the founder,

Pompilius of the tranquil reign, or else
Tarquin the splendid, or Cato who by death

Set such an example, as Regulus also did,
Or men like Scaurus, or like Paulus who was

So generous with his very life in the time
When Hannibal was winning. Which of these

Takes precedence in my praise? And also there's
Fabricius, and long-haired Curius,

Camillus whom the austerity of the farm
His fathers also tilled made ready for war.

As in the secret way of time a great
Tree grows, so grows Marcellus' fame; and as

The moon at night outshines the other lights,
The light of the Julian constellation shines

Far brighter than the light of other lights.
O son of Saturn, Father Jupiter,

Guardian as you are of all things human,
May Caesar reign, your second, guarded by you,

And guardian in his turn may Caesar guard
His Romans from all their foes, whether they be

The Parthians menacing Latium, the Indians, or
The Seres beyond the borders to the East.

te minor laetum reget aequus orbem:
tu gravi curru quaties Olympum,
tu parum castis inimica mittes
    fulmina lucis.

May Caesar with justice rule, second to you,
Across the regions of the whole wide world,

While Jupiter's heavy chariot shakes the sky
And Jupiter's lightning strikes the polluted woods.

i.13

Cum tu, Lydia, Telephi
  cervicem roseam, cerea Telephi
laudas bracchia, vae, meum
  fervens difficili bile tumet iecur.

Tum nec mens mihi nec color
  certa sede manent, umor et in genas
furtim labitur, arguens
  quam lentis penitus macerer ignibus.

Uror, seu tibi candidos
  turparunt umeros immodicae mero
rixae, sive puer furens
  impressit memorem dente labris notam.

Non, si me satis audias,
  speres perpetuum dulcia barbare
laedentem oscula quae Venus
  quinta parte sui nectaris imbuit.

Felices ter et amplius
  quos irrupta tenet copula nec malis
divulsus querimoniis
  suprema citius solvet amor die.

Lydia, when you praise your Telephus,
"His beautiful rosy neck," "his beautiful arms,"
Your praise of Telephus throws me into confusion,
My mind is all unsettled, my heart swells up,

The tears in my eyes are the visible evidence
Of the fire that burns inside me and torments me.
I suffer this way whether I think the bruise
That mars your snow-white shoulder is the sign

Of a lovers' quarrel brought on by too much wine
Or the mark on your lip the mark of his savage kiss.
If you listened to me you wouldn't give your trust
To one who would so barbarously treat

The lips that Venus imbued with essence of nectar.
Those lovers are happy and more than happy who
Are peacefully bound together in amity.
Love will not part such lovers until death parts them.

O navis, referent in mare te novi
fluctus. O quid agis! Fortiter occupa
   portum. Nonne vides ut
     nudum remigio latus

et malus celeri saucius Africo
antemnaeque gemant, ac sine funibus
   vix durare carinae
     possint imperiosius

aequor? Non tibi sunt integra lintea,
non di quos iterum pressa voces malo.
   Quamvis Pontica pinus,
     silvae filia nobilis,

iactes et genus et nomen inutile,
nil pictis timidus navita puppibus
   fidit. Tu, nisi ventis
     debes ludibrium, cave.

Nuper sollicitum quae mihi taedium,
nunc desiderium curaque non levis,
   interfusa nitentis
     vites aequora Cycladas.

i.14 / *To the Republic*

O ship, O battered ship, the backward running waves

Are taking you out to sea again! Oh what to do?

Oh don't you see? Oh make for port! The wind's gone wild!

Your sails are torn! Your mast is shaking! Your oars are gone!

Your onboard gods gone overboard! How long, how long

Can the eggshell hull so frail hold out? O ship so proud,

Your famous name, your gilded stern, your polished decks,

Your polished brass, so useless now, O storm's play thing,

O ship my care, beware, beware the Cyclades!

i.15

Pastor cum traheret per freta navibus
Idaeis Helenen perfidus hospitam,
ingrato celeris obruit otio
    ventos, ut caneret fera

Nereus fata: "Mala ducis avi domum
quam multo repetet Graecia milite,
coniurata tuas rumpere nuptias
    et regnum Priami vetus.

Heu, heu, quantus equis, quantus adest viris
sudor! Quanta moves funera Dardanae
genti! Iam galeam Pallas et aegida
    currusque et rabiem parat.

Nequiquam Veneris praesidio ferox
pectes caesariem grataque feminis
imbelli cithara carmina divides;
    nequiquam thalamo gravis

hastas et calami spicula Cnosii
vitabis strepitumque et celerem sequi
Aiacem: tamen (heu serus!) adulteros
    crines pulvere collines.

Non Laërtiaden, exitium tuae
gentis, non Pylium Nestora respicis?
Urgent impavidi te Salaminius
    Teucer, te Sthenelus sciens

pugnae, sive opus est imperitare equis,
non auriga piger. Merionen quoque
nosces. Ecce furit te reperire atrox
    Tydides melior patre,

As Paris, beautiful treacherous shepherd youth,
Betrayer of Menelaus, fled with his Helen
Over the waves to safety, or so they thought,
Nereus, prophetic god, stilled the sea-winds,

And, becoming a sea bird, sang of things to come.
The little boat, becalmed, rocked in the water.
"Bad luck for Troy that this adventure brings.
The woman you are bringing home will bring

Against your home how many Grecian heroes
Determined to undo what you have done
And to bring down the city of your father.
Alas, what dolorous work for men and horses

You are the cause of. Already I see the goddess
Pallas Athena as she is putting on
Her glittering helmet and as she is getting ready
Her shield and shining car, preparing her rage.

What good will it do to sit in your lady's chamber,
Venus's hero, combing your beautiful hair
And playing a tune on the cithara, of the sort
That women like? What good will it do to try,

In a palace room, to avoid the noise of battle,
The spears and arrows and Ajax in pursuit?
It won't be long, although, alas, too late,
Before your beautiful hair gets dirty enough

When you lie down in the dirt. Haven't you heard
Of Laertes' son, the scourge of the Trojan people?
Haven't you heard of Nestor? And don't you know
That Salaminian Teucer, brother of Ajax,

Deterred by nothing, is on the hunt for you?
And, undeterred, Sthenelus too, and he,
Tydeus' terrible son, more terrible than
His terrible father, is hot to hunt you down?

quem tu, cervus uti vallis in altera
visum parte lupum graminis immemor,
sublimi fugies mollis anhelitu,
   non hoc pollicitus tuae.

Iracunda diem proferet Ilio
matronisque Phrygum classis Achilleï;
post certas hiemes uret Achaïcus
   ignis Iliacas domos."

And you, like a grazing deer that when it sees
A wolf on the other side of the valley coming
Forgets to graze and runs as fast as it can,
Head back and panting hard, heart throbbing, you

Will run away as fast as you can, head back
And panting hard, how much unlike how you
Had promised her that you were going to be,
Heart throb, with Helen in the palace chamber."

O matre pulchra filia pulchrior,
quem criminosis cumque voles modum
   pones iambis, sive flamma
      sive mari libet Hadriano.

Non Dindymene, non adytis quatit
mentem sacerdotum incola Pythius,
   non Liber aeque, non acuta
      sic geminant Corybantes aera,

tristes ut irae, quas neque Noricus
deterret ensis nec mare naufragum
   nec saevus ignis nec tremendo
      Iuppiter ipse ruens tumultu.

Fertur Prometheus, addere principi
limo coactus particulam undique
   desectam, et insani leonis
      vim stomacho apposuisse nostro.

Irae Thyesten exitio gravi
stravere et altis urbibus ultimae
   stetere causae cur perirent
      funditus, imprimeretque muris

hostile aratrum exercitus insolens.
Compesce mentem! Me quoque pectoris
   temptavit in dulci iuventa
      fervor et in celeres iambos

misit furentem; nunc ego mitibus
mutare quaero tristia, dum mihi
   fias recantatis amica
      opprobriis animumque reddas.

O daughter more beautiful than her beautiful mother,
Do what you will to put an end to those
Slanderous verses I wrote—why don't you burn them,
Or let the thirsty Adriatic drink them?

Not Dindymene, not the god who in
His shrine at Pytho brings the priestesses
To frenzy, neither Bacchus nor the shrilling
Cymbals in the Corybantic dance

Can shake the soul as human anger shakes it,
Which neither fire nor sword represses nor
Does ship-destroying storm nor Jupiter's
Punishing wrath ruining down on the world.

It is said that when Prometheus was assigned
The task of making each of us what we are,
He put into each one of us something of
Each other creature that there is in nature.

He put into our human hearts the rage
Of the lion feeding insanely on his prey.
It was the rage of Atreus that brought
Thyestes to the feast where he ate his children.

Rage thrills in the heart of the victor as he drives
His jubilant plow over the rubble of cities.
Restrain your rage. Raging in youth I wrote
Those angry verses, wrote them down and sent them.

How gladly would I change them now if you
As gladly gave me back your friendship and
Your all-forgiving heart, since, Helena, now
I do repent and solemnly recant.

Velox amoenum saepe Lucretilem
mutat Lycaeo Faunus et igneam
 defendit aestatem capellis
  usque meis pluviosque ventos.

Impune tutum per nemus arbutos
quaerunt latentis et thyma deviae
 olentis uxores mariti,
  nec viridis metuunt colubras

nec Martialis haediliae lupos,
utcumque dulci, Tyndari, fistula
 valles et Usticae cubantis
  levia personuere saxa.

Di me tuentur, dis pietas mea
et Musa cordi est; hinc tibi copia
 manabit ad plenum benigno
  ruris honorum opulenta cornu.

Hic in reducta valle Caniculae
vitabis aestus, et fide Teïa
 dices laborantis in uno
  Penelopen vitreamque Circen;

hic innocentis pocula Lesbii
duces sub umbra, nec Semeleïus
 cum Marte confundet Thyoneus
  proelia, nec metues protervum

suspecta Cyrum, ne male dispari
incontinentis iniciat manus
 et scindat haerentem coronam
  crinibus immeritamque vestem.

Sometimes Faunus comes from Arcady
To fair Lucretilis, and while he's here
Sees to it that my goats are sheltered from
The summer heat and from the wind and rain.

Tyndaris, when this place falls under the spell
Of the rocks and hills of Ustica echoing
The sound of Faunus playing upon his pipe,
The wives of the rank male goat then feeling easy

Can wander through the woods in safety searching
For thyme and for arbutus where they hide,
Nor do the kids have anything to fear
From snakes nor from Mars' favorite, the wolf.

The gods protect me here because they know
That I and my Muse are ever devout and faithful.
And here, for you, from the horn of plenty flow
All the good things of our local fields and vines.

Here you can shade yourself from the heat of summer,
Singing a song about Penelope
And Circe of the glassy sea, and how
Both of them loved the wandering Ulysses.

Here you will sit, under these guardian plane trees,
Tasting the mild innocent wine of Lesbos;
Here Mars and Bacchus, Semele's child, will never
Contend to make trouble; and, untroubled here,

Protected, here in the garden, under these trees,
You will have nothing to fear from jealous Cyrus,
Tearing your dress, or disarranging your hair,
Pawing you with his cruel offending hands.

i.18

Nullam, Vare, sacra vite prius severis arborem
circa mite solum Tiburis et moenia Catili;
siccis omnia nam dura deus proposuit neque
mordaces aliter diffugiunt sollicitudines.
Quis post vina gravem militiam aut pauperiem crepat?
Quis non te potius, Bacche pater, teque decens Venus?
Ac ne quis modici transiliat munera Liberi,
Centaurea monet cum Lapithis rixa super mero
debellata, monet Sithoniis non levis Euhius,
cum fas atque nefas exiguo fine libidinum
discernunt avidi. Non ego te, candide Bassareu,
invitum quatiam nec variis obsita frondibus
sub divum rapiam. Saeva tene cum Berecyntio
cornu tympana, quae subsequitur caecus Amor sui
et tollens vacuam plus nimio Gloria verticem
arcanique Fides prodiga, perlucidior vitro.

For planting in the rich Tiburtine soil
Upon the slopes of Mount Catillus, Varus,
Favor no plant before the sacred vine.
Bacchus commands that everything be hard
For him who abstains from wine, and Bacchus says
The troubles that wear away our days are not
Made easier by any other means.
After a drink or two who is it who
Complains about the hardships of his lot—
His poverty, or his service in the army?
Who fails to praise you then, O father Bacchus?
Who fails to praise you too, O queen of love?
And yet there is a lesson in the example
Of the fight between the Centaurs and the Lapiths,
That went so far too far at the drunken banquet.
And there's another in the Sithonian drinkers
Who think they tell right from wrong by squinting along
The disappearing line libidinous desire
Draws on the wet bartop. I would not dare
To stir you up, O Bacchus, against your will,
Nor will I be the one to betray to the light
The secret signs that you have covered over
In grape and ivy leaves. Bacchus, repress
The cymbal and the Berecynthian horn
And those who revel in that raucous music:
Blind love that has no eyes but for itself;
Vain Glory with its vacant head held high;
And barfly Faithlessness whose promiscuous tongue
Spills all its secrets into promiscuous ears.

Mater saeva Cupidinum
   Thebanaeque iubet me Semelae puer
et lasciva Licentia
   finitis animum reddere amoribus.

Urit me Glycerae nitor,
   splendentis Pario marmore purius;
urit grata protervitas
   et vultus nimium lubricus aspici.

In me tota ruens Venus
   Cyprum deseruit, nec patitur Scythas
et versis animosum equis
   Parthum dicere, nec quae nihil attinent.

Hic vivum mihi caespitem, hic
   verbenas, pueri, ponite turaque
bimi cum patera meri:
   mactata veniet lenior hostia.

i.19 / *Glycera*

The pitiless mother of all the amorini,
And Bacchus, Semele's son, and the lascivious

Goddess Licentia, all of them, all,
Bring back to me all at once the forgotten loves

I thought I had forgotten all about,
For I have fallen in love with Glycera's body,

Smoother than shining marble is shining and smooth,
And with her way of behaving, so wanton and pleasing,

And with the bold lubricious look on her face,
That makes you lose your footing to look at her.

Venus is coming from Cyprus to ruin me,
And now I cannot sing about the wars

Against the Scythians, the Parthians, or any
Other such things that are irrelevant.

Come, boys, my slaves, set up an altar here,
Of grassy turf, adorn it with leaves and branches,

Perfume the air with incense and set out
A bowl of last year's wine unmixed with water.

Perhaps if I offer a sacrifice to Venus
Venus will be less cruel when she comes.

i.20

Vile potabis modicis Sabinum
cantharis, Graeca quod ego ipse testa
conditum levi, datus in theatro
    cum tibi plausus,

care Maecenas eques, ut paterni
fluminis ripae simul et iocosa
redderet laudes tibi Vaticani
    montis imago.

Caecubum et prelo domitam Caleno
tu bibes uvam: mea nec Falernae
temperant vites neque Formiani
    pocula colles.

Maecenas, when you come to visit me
You will share with me from ordinary cups

The Sabine wine my household has to offer,
The local table wine of the neighborhood.

I put it up myself in a Grecian jug
On the very day, dear friend, when you came back,

Recovered at last from almost having died,
To the Campus Martius and to great applause

That echoed from the banks of your native Tiber
And joyfully from the Vatican Hills beyond.

Maecenas, you have better wines at home
Than my poor cups have ever known the taste of.

You have the Calenian wine, the Caecuban wine,
The Falernian, and the wine from the Formian Hills.

Dianam tenerae dicite virgines,
intonsum, pueri, dicite Cynthium
Latonamque supremo
dilectam penitus Iovi.

Vos laetam fluviis et nemorum coma,
quaecumque aut gelido prominet Algido,
nigris aut Erymanthi
silvis aut viridis Cragi;

vos Tempe totidem tollite laudibus
natalemque, mares, Delon Apollonis,
insignemque pharetra
fraternaque umerum lyra.

Hic bellum lacrimosum, hic miseram famem
pestemque a populo et principe Caesare in
Persas atque Britannos
vestra motus aget prece.

Let the young women praise Diana, and let
The young men praise unshorn Apollo, and let
    Them praise Latona whom
    Jupiter deeply loved.

Young women praise Diana who loves the streams
And loves the bright green groves among the black
    Erymanthian woods and on
    Cold Algidus' side;

Young men praise Tempe and praise the island Delos,
The birthplace of Apollo, and praise Apollo's
    Shoulder that wears the quiver
    And the lyre his brother made.

Apollo guard us from the wretched plague,
From hunger and from war the cause of tears,
    And bring them down upon
    The Parthians and Britons.

i.22

Integer vitae scelerisque purus
non eget Mauris iaculis neque arcu
nec venenatis gravida sagittis,
    Fusce, pharetra,

sive per Syrtis iter aestuosas
sive facturus per inhospitalem
Caucasum vel quae loca fabulosus
    lambit Hydaspes.

Namque me silva lupus in Sabina,
dum meam canto Lalagen et ultra
terminum curis vagor expeditis,
    fugit inermem;

quale portentum neque militaris
Daunias latis alit aesculetis
nec Iubae tellus generat, leonum
    arida nutrix.

Pone me pigris ubi nulla campis
arbor aestiva recreatur aura,
quod latus mundi nebulae malusque
    Iuppiter urget;

pone sub curru nimium propinqui
solis in terra domibus negata:
dulce ridentem Lalagen amabo,
    dulce loquentem.

The upright man whose conscience is perfectly clear
Can journey anywhere, unarmed, untroubled,
Whether it be the burning sands of Sidra,
Near where the quicksand waits for you under the sea,

Or the frozen Caucasus, or the fabled place
There are so many monster stories about,
Washed by the sinister River Hydaspes. For instance,
Fuscus, there was the summer day when I

Went out of my Sabine house, in the afternoon,
And wandered in the woods beyond my farm,
Singing my song about my Lalage,
Carefree, alone, and utterly unprotected,

When suddenly there was a wolf, more frightening than
The wolves in the oak tree forests of Apulia
Or the lions for which Numidia is famous—
And the wolf ran away from *me*! So let me tell you:

Set me down anywhere, say in a place
That's entirely lifeless, where not a single tree
Responds to any breeze, a place the gods
Have cursed with evil stagnant mists forever,

Or leave me where the sun comes near the earth
Too hot for any man to be able to dwell there,
And I will nevertheless go right on singing
My ardent song in praise of Lalage.

i.23

Vitas inuleo me similis, Chloë,
quaerenti pavidam montibus aviis
   matrem non sine vano
     aurarum et siluae metu.

Nam seu mobilibus veris inhorruit
adventus foliis, seu virides rubum
   dimovere lacertae,
     et corde et genibus tremit.

Atqui non ego te tigris ut aspera
Gaetulusve leo frangere persequor:
   tandem desine matrem
     tempestiva sequi viro.

Chloë, it is as if
  You were but a little fawn
Needlessly fearful of every
  Littlest breeze that stirs,

Ready to run as far
  Away as it possibly can,
Seeking its timid mother
  Anywhere but here

Where its heart beats fast and it trembles
  In every limb for any
Slightest shimmer or shiver
  Of newly opening leaf,

Signs of the spring beginning,
  Or if a lizard's foot
Disturbs a single twig.
  Chloë, I am neither

A lion nor a tiger;
  I have no wish to hurt you;
Do not run to your mother;
  Now is the time for love.

Quis desiderio sit pudor aut modus
tam cari capitis? Praecipe lugubris
cantus, Melpomene, cui liquidam pater
    vocem cum cithara dedit.

Ergo Quintilium perpetuus sopor
urget? Cui Pudor et Iustitiae soror,
incorrupta Fides, nudaque Veritas
    quando ullum inveniet parem?

Multis ille bonis flebilis occidit,
nulli flebilior quam tibi, Vergili.
Tu frustra pius heu non ita creditum
    poscis Quintilium deos.

Quid? Si Threïcio blandius Orpheo
auditam moderere arboribus fidem,
num vanae redeat sanguis imagini,
    quam virga semel horrida,

non lenis precibus fata recludere,
nigro compulerit Mercurius gregi?
Durum: sed levius fit patientia
    quicquid corrigere est nefas.

How should this grief be properly put into words?
Melpomene, to whom the Father gave
The voice that to the music of the lyre
Flows out in mournful measure, teach me the art.

Can it be true that Quintilius lies in the sleep
That goes on without ever ending? Where then will Justice,
And Faith, the sister of Justice, and Decency,
And Truth that needs no ornament, find his equal?

Virgil, many are they who mourn for him,
But none like you who mourn so, ceaselessly.
Your pious grief, alas, can never persuade
The gods to alter the terms that gave him life.

Suppose that you were able to play the lyre
Even more skillfully than Orpheus played it,
Causing the very trees to listen to him,
What good would it do? Could the music restore

Blood to the veins of the empty shade of one
Who has died? How could the music persuade the god
To open the door he has shut, and shut once and for all,
The god whose horrid wand shepherds the dead

To where they are going down there to be shut away?
It is hard. But all of this must be endured,
And by endurance what can never be changed
Will be at last made easier in the heart.

i.25

Parcius iunctas quatiunt fenestras
iactibus crebris iuvenes protervi,
nec tibi somnos adimunt, amatque
    ianua limen,

quae prius multum facilis movebat
cardines. Audis minus et minus iam:
"Me tuo longas pereunte noctes
    Lydia, dormis?"

Invicem moechos anus arrogantis
flebis in solo levis angiportu,
Thracio bacchante magis sub inter-
    lunia vento,

cum tibi flagrans amor et libido,
quae solet matres furiare equorum,
saeviet circa iecur ulcerosum,
    non sine questu,

laeta quod pubes hedera virenti
gaudeat pulla magis atque myrto,
aridas frondes hiemis sodali
    dedicet Euro.

It happens less and less often, now, that you
Wake up to hear the sound of gravel thrown

Against your shuttered windows in the night.
It's very seldom, now, that you can't sleep

The whole night through. There used to be a time
The hinges of the door to your house moved ever so

Easily back and forth. Not anymore.
It's very seldom, Lydia, now, that you

Can hear a lover out in the dark complain:
"O Lydia, Lydia, why are you sound asleep

While all night long I suffer in the alley?"
You're going to have your turn out there alone,

Old crone in the nighttime alley weeping, weeping
Over your faithless boyfriends while the North Wind

Coming down from the Thracian cold blows ever
Louder and louder through the dark of the moon,

And ulcerating lust such as the lust
That tortures the mare in heat tortures your heart.

Out there in the night you'll moan that all the young men
Prefer the lustrous ivy and lustrous myrtle

To the withered leaves that winter's companion the cold
Wind causes to scatter and scrape along the alley.

i.26

Musis amicus tristitiam et metus
tradam protervis in mare Creticum
 portare ventis, quis sub Arcto
  rex gelidae metuatur orae,

quid Tiridaten terreat, unice
securus. O quae fontibus integris
 gaudes, apricos necte flores,
  necte meo Lamiae coronam,

Pipleï dulcis. Nil sine te mei
prosunt honores: hunc fidibus novis,
 hunc Lesbio sacrare plectro
  teque tuasque decet sorores.

Because the Muses favor me and love me,
As far as I'm concerned let the wild winds carry
All sadness and trepidation far away.

Who cares what king in some cold country scares us,
Or what some other king or would-be king
Himself is scared of? Who cares about these things?

O Muse who loves the fountains, help me to fashion
Metrical garlands to celebrate my friend,
Whose virtues are a cause for celebration.

Without your help our praises are as nothing.
Grant us new harmonies and grant new measures
To guarantee the celebration forever.

Natis in usum laetitiae scyphis
pugnare Thracum est: tollite barbarum
   morem, verecundumque Bacchum
     sanguineis prohibete rixis.

Vino et lucernis Medus acinaces
immane quantum discrepat: impium
   lenite clamorem, sodales,
     et cubito remanete presso.

Vultis severi me quoque sumere
partem Falerni? Dicat Opuntiae
   frater Megillae, quo beatus
     vulnere, qua pereat sagitta.

Cessat voluntas? Non alia bibam
mercede. Quae te cumque domat Venus,
   non erubescendis adurit
     ignibus ingenuoque semper

amore peccas. Quicquid habes, age,
depone tutis auribus. A miser,
   quanta laborabas Charybdi,
     digne puer meliore flamma!

Quae saga, quis te solvere Thessalis
magus venenis, quis poterit deus?
   Vix illigatum te triformi
     Pegasus expediet Chimaera.

These drinking goblets, meant for pleasure, are
Not meant to brawl with, as the Thracians do.
Let us behave as Bacchus means us to.
Brandishing swords is out of keeping here,

To say the least, in the lamplit banquet room,
And brandishing insults too. Let's take it easy,
Let's have a peaceful quiet drinking party,
Good friends together, having a good time.

But don't ask me to have a cup of wine
Until Megylla's brother tells the truth
About the pains of love he struggles with,
So wounded, in such bliss. I'll drink no wine

Until he will consent to tell me who.
You won't say who? Whoever she is, no matter;
You need not blush as if you'd caught on fire;
I'm sure whoever you choose is worthy of you.

Whoever she is, then, tell me in my ear,
Which you can trust with secrets, tell me, who?
—O miserable! If it is *she*, then *you*—
Charybdis reels around you—you flail in the water.

Where is the witch or wizard able to save you?
Where is the god? Enraptured drowning child,
Bellerophon and Pegasus who killed
The triple-formed Chimera, not even they

Could set you free from such a one as she.

i.28

Te maris et terrae numeroque carentis harenae
    mensorem cohibent, Archyta,
pulveris exigui prope litus parva Matinum
    munera, nec quicquam tibi prodest

aërias temptasse domos animoque rotundum
    percurrisse polum morituro.
Occidit et Pelopis genitor, conviva deorum,
    Tithonusque remotus in auras

et Iovis arcanis Minos admissus, habentque
    Tartara Panthoïden iterum Orco
demissum, quamvis clipeo Troiana refixo
    tempora testatus nihil ultra

nervos atque cutem morti concesserat atrae,
    iudice te non sordidus auctor
naturae verique. Sed omnis una manet nox,
    et calcanda semel via leti.

i.28   /   *A Beach near Tarentum*

A traveler ashore on a beach near Tarentum happens upon the
grave of the Pythagorean philosopher Archytas:

What good does it do you, Archytas, confined as you are
To this little heap of earth on this lonely strand

Beside the sea? Archytas, you measured the earth
And counted all the uncountable grains of sand

There are on the beach. What good does it do you now?
What good does it do that once upon a time

You went out exploring the houses of gods in the sky,
Adventuring in your mind round heaven's rotunda?

What good does it do, now death has taken your measure?
The father of Pelops fell, though he was once

Convivial at the banquet of the gods,
And Tithonus fell, whom heaven had taken up.

Minos, too, whom Jupiter had conferred with,
And Pythagoras, having chosen the very shield

That belonged to Euphorbus the long-dead Trojan hero
From a hundred other shields of long-dead heroes,

Thought he, Pythagoras, must have been he, Euphorbus,
Back in a former life. And so he died

A second time, and therefore he was sent
A second time to Orcus down below,

This time for good. Pythagoreans think,
Who think Pythagoras by far the best

Witness there ever was to truth and nature,
He must have defeated death at least that once.

Dant alios Furiae torvo spectacula Marti,
    exitio est avidum mare nautis;
mixta senum ac iuvenum densentur funera, nullum
    saeva caput Proserpina fugit.

Me quoque devexi rapidus comes Orionis
    Illyricis Notus obruit undis.
At tu, nauta, vagae ne parce malignus harenae
    ossibus et capiti inhumato

particulam dare: sic, quodcumque minabitur Eurus
    fluctibus Hesperiis, Venusinae
plectantur silvae te sospite, multaque merces,
    unde potest, tibi defluat aequo

ab Iove Neptunoque sacri custode Tarenti.
    Neglegis immeritis nocituram
postmodo te natis fraudem committere? Fors et
    debita iura vicesque superbae

But no. Be sure of this. The dark is final
Once and for all, body and soul, for all,

And all must go there by the path of death.
Some are presented by the Furies as

A spectacle for the pleasure of savage Mars;
The hungry sea devours the drowning sailor;

Old and young jostle together on their way down;
No one is spared by cruel Proserpina.

The voice of the unburied corpse of a sailor, nearby on the
beach, speaks to the traveler:

I too have perished. I too was one who drowned.
Notus, bad wind confederate of Orion,

Brought on the storm that overwhelmed my boat,
And so it was I died. O traveler,

O passerby, do not refuse a few
Handfuls of sand to cover up my corpse

Exposed unburied here on the lonely beach.
Three handfuls given, then no matter how

The surf is raised up by the great storm wind,
May you be safe and may the harmless storm

Exhaust its rage upon the Venusian woods
Far inland. May good fortune come to you

From Jupiter and from Neptune, god of Tarentum.
If you refuse, have you thought about the curse?

It may be you who needs these rites someday,
And they may be disdained. O passerby,

te maneant ipsum: precibus non linquar inultis,
teque piacula nulla resolvent.
Quamquam festinas, non est mora longa; licebit
iniecto ter pulvere curras.

I will not unavenged unburied be.
No penitential offering later on

Will help you then. Therefore pause but a moment
To give three handfuls of sand. And go on your way.

Icci, beatis nunc Arabum invides
gazis et acrem militiam paras
   non ante devictis Sabaeae
     regibus, horribilique Medo

nectis catenas? Quae tibi virginum
sponso necato barbara serviet?
   Puer quis ex aula capillis
     ad cyathum statuetur unctis,

doctus sagittas tendere Sericas
arcu paterno? Quis neget arduis
   pronos relabi posse rivos
     montibus et Tiberim reverti,

cum tu coëmptos undique nobilis
libros Panaeti Socraticum et domum
   mutare loricis Hiberis,
     pollicitus meliora, tendis?

i.29 / *To Iccius*

Is it true that you have your eye on
  Getting your share of the rich
    Exotic treasure that Eastern

Kingdoms promise the victor?
  True that you're busy preparing
    To bring down war on the heads of

Whoever is left unconquered
  In all of exotic Arabia?
    True that you're already linking

The chains to shackle your prisoners,
  Indian, maybe, Chinese, or
    Some other nation like that?

Who is the maiden who'll be your
  Slave after pitiless you
    Have slain her young lover in battle?

Who is the youth, brought up in
  Some royal Eastern palace
    And taught by his father the deadly

Art of the bow and arrow,
  Who'll stand by your chair and be your
    Perfumed attentive cupbearer?

Maybe the Tiber and all
  Other rivers will suddenly turn
    Around in their courses and run

Right back uphill to their sources,
  If you turn around and trade in
    The books you love so dearly,

Panaetius, Plato, and such,
  To put on Spanish armor
    And go off to be a soldier.

O Venus, regina Cnidi Paphique,
sperne dilectam Cypron et vocantis
ture te multo Glycerae decoram
    transfer in aedem.

Fervidus tecum puer et solutis
Gratiae zonis properentque nymphae
et parum comis sine te Iuventas
    Mercuriusque.

i.30 / *To Venus*

Venus, Queen of Cnidos and of Paphos,
Leave your island, Cyprus, which you love,
And come to Glycera's house, which she has made,
With incense and with prayer, a shrine to Venus.

And bring your child, the amorous boy, and bring
The half-clad Graces too, and bring the Nymphs,
And Mercury, and with them lovely Youth,
Whose loveliness without you is as nothing.

Quid dedicatum poscit Apollinem
vates? Quid orat, de patera novum
  fundens liquorem? Non opimae
    Sardiniae segetes feracis,

non aestuosae grata Calabriae
armenta, non aurum aut ebur Indicum,
  non rura quae Liris quieta
    mordet aqua taciturnus amnis.

Premant Calena falce quibus dedit
Fortuna vitem, dives et aureis
  mercator exsiccet culillis
    vina Syra reparata merce,

dis carus ipsis, quippe ter et quater
anno revisens aequor Atlanticum
  impune. Me pascunt olivae,
    me cichorea levesque malvae.

Frui paratis et valido mihi,
Latoë, dones ac, precor, integra
  cum mente, nec turpem senectam
    degere nec cithara carentem.

i.31 / *A Prayer*

What shall I ask for from the god Apollo
As on his day I pour the new wine out,

Here in his temple, at the petition time?
Neither for gold nor Indian ivory

Nor for the lavish harvests of Sardinia,
Nor for the herds of grazing cattle that make

The Calabrian landscape such a delight to see,
Nor for the fields whose edges the Liris River

Grazes upon as it quietly moves along.
Let those to whom the privilege has been given

Prune their vines that grow the Calenian wine
The merchant pours out into his golden wine glass

Which he has bought with what he got for trading
With what he brought from Syria this year—

He who's so favored by all the gods that he
Can go out upon the dangerous Atlantic

Time after time and come back safe and sound.
But as for me, my simple meal consists

Of chicory and mallow from the garden
And olives from the little olive tree.

Apollo grant that I be satisfied
With what I have as what I ought to have,

And that I live my old age out with honor,
In health of mind and body, doing my work.

Poscimus, si quid vacui sub umbra
lusimus tecum quod et hunc in annum
vivat et pluris, age dic Latinum,
    barbite, carmen,

Lesbio primum modulate civi,
qui ferox bello tamen inter arma,
sive iactatam religarat udo
    litore navim,

Liberum et Musas Veneremque et illi
semper haerentem puerum canebat,
et Lycum nigris oculis nigroque
    crine decorum.

O decus Phoebi et dapibus supremi
grata testudo Iovis, o laborum
dulce lenimen, mihi cumque salve
    rite vocanti.

Pray for a new song. You and I together
Under the trees in the shade, have played such songs
As could live beyond the end of the year, and longer,
   O lyre, O tortoise shell,

First stringed and tuned to make the beautiful music
Alcaeus played in the Grecian battle camp,
And, having survived the storm and brought his boat
   Safe to the wave-drenched beach,

Played on the beach his songs of Bacchus and
Of Venus and the child who clings to her,
And dark-haired dark-eyed Lycus whom he loved.
   Let us play a Roman song.

O instrument of Phoebus Apollo's favor,
O gladly heard at Jupiter's table itself,
O medicine of sorrows, now bring forth
   The music I invoke.

i.33

Albi, ne doleas plus nimio memor
immitis Glycerae neu miserabilis
decantes elegos, cur tibi iunior
    laesa praeniteat fide.

Insignem tenui fronte Lycorida
Cyri torret amor, Cyrus in asperam
declinat Pholoën; sed prius Apulis
    iungentur capreae lupis

quam turpi Pholoë peccet adultero.
Sic visum Veneri, cui placet imparis
formas atque animos sub iuga aënea
    saevo mittere cum ioco.

Ipsum me melior cum peteret Venus,
grata detinuit compede Myrtale
libertina, fretis acrior Hadriae
    curvantis Calabros sinus.

Albius, don't feel
  So sorry for yourself,
Going on the way you do
  With your lovelorn love songs, just
Because Glycera has fallen
  For somebody younger than you.
Lycoris of the beautiful
  Forehead burns with love
For Cyrus, and Cyrus burns
  With love for Pholoë,
But a doe is just about
  As likely to mate with a wolf
As Pholoë with him.

It is the will of Venus,
  Who has a lot of fun
With the cruel joke of putting
  Like and unlike together
In the same brazen yoke.
  Thus I, although a better
Finds me the object of
  Her unrequited passion,
Find I'm bound by passion
  To slave-born Myrtale,
A woman stormier than
  The stormy waters off
The wild Calabrian shore.

i.34

Parcus deorum cultor et infrequens
insanientis dum sapientiae
  consultus erro, nunc retrorsum
    vela dare atque iterare cursus

cogor relictos. Namque Diespiter,
igni corusco nubila dividens
  plerumque, per purum tonantis
    egit equos volucremque currum;

quo bruta tellus et vaga flumina
quo Styx et invisi horrida Taenari
  sedes Atlanteusque finis
    concutitur. Valet ima summis

mutare et insignem attenuat deus,
obscura promens; hinc apicem rapax
  Fortuna cum stridore acuto
    sustulit, hic posuisse gaudet.

Sparing and but perfunctory in my devotions,
Going my own way, wandering in my learnèd
Well-considered folly, now I must turn about,

And change my course, and sail for home and safety.
Jupiter, whose thunder and whose lightning
Require the clouds, just now, this minute, drove

His thundering chariot and his thundering horses
Right straight across a perfectly cloudless sky,
Unsettling streams and shaking the heavy ground

All the way down to the river Styx and out
To the end of the earth beyond Taenarus' seat,
Where Atlas holds up the sky upon his shoulders.

Oh yes, the god has power. Oh yes, he can
Raise up the low and bring the high things down.
Fortune's wings rustle as the choice is made.

i.35

O diva, gratum quae regis Antium,
praesens vel imo tollere de gradu
   mortale corpus vel superbos
      vertere funeribus triumphos,

te pauper ambit sollicita prece
ruris colonus, te dominam aequoris,
   quicumque Bithyna lacessit
      Carpathium pelagus carina;

te Dacus asper, te profugi Scythae
urbesque gentesque et Latium ferox
   regumque matres barbarorum et
      purpurei metuunt tyranni,

iniurioso ne pede proruas
stantem columnam, neu populus frequens
   ad arma cessantis, ad arma
      concitet imperiumque frangat.

Te semper anteit saeva Necessitas,
clavos trabalis et cuneos manu
   gestans aëna, nec severus
      uncus abest liquidumque plumbum.

Te Spes et albo rara Fides colit
velata panno, nec comitem abnegat,
   utcumque mutata potentis
      veste domos inimica linquis.

At vulgus infidum et meretrix retro
periura cedit, diffugiunt cadis
   cum faece siccatis amici,
      ferre iugum pariter dolosi.

O goddess whose shrine is lovely Antium,
Your presence has the power to raise the low,
Bring down the high, and make a triumphal march
Of what had been a funeral procession.

The poor man on his farm solicits your favor
With anxious prayers; the sailor prays to you,
Queen of the waters, on his Bithynian boat,
Wherever he is, out on the wild Aegean.

The uncouth Dacian, the nomad Scythian,
All towns and cities, wherever they are, send up
Their prayers to you; tyrants in royal purple,
Barbarian kings and their imperious mothers,

All of them, every last one of them, living in fear
That one of these days you might knock the supporting column
Out from under the roof of the house of power;
They live in fear that one of these days the rabble

Might stir up the citizens, crying "To arms! To arms!"
And bring the whole structure down upon their heads.
Walking before you, as she always does,
Is the giant goddess cruel Necessity;

In her iron hands she carries a spike, and a wedge,
A clamp, a hook, and a pail of molten lead.
And when offended Fortune takes her leave
From the sorrowing household of some powerful man,

Then Hope and Faith in ceremonial clothes
Attend upon her and make their departure too;
And the fickle whores and hangers-on of power,
And the fair-weather family friends, once they have drained

The wine-jars of the house to the utmost dregs,
Are scattered far and wide, unwilling to share
The burden of the trouble that has come.
Oh keep our Caesar safe when he sets forth

Serves iturum Caesarem in ultimos
orbis Britannos et iuvenum recens
    examen, Eois timendum
        partibus Oceanoque rubro.

Eheu, cicatricum et sceleris pudet
fratrumque. Quid nos dura refugimus
    aetas? Quid intactum nefasti
        liquimus? Unde manum iuventus

metu deorum continuit? Quibus
pepercit aris? O utinam nova
    incude diffingas retusum in
        Massagetas Arabasque ferrum!

To invade that savage island of the Britons
Out at the end of the earth; protect our army
Now setting out to terrify the tribes
That dwell in the East along the Red Sea shore.

Alas, our deeds have brought us down to shame—
Brother against brother, the wounds, oh, all the bloodshed!
What has this generation left undone?
What crimes against ourselves have our young men

Held back their hands from doing, for fear of the gods?
Fortuna, may our blunted swords be forged
Anew upon new anvils and be turned
Against the Massagetae and the Arabs.

i.36

Et ture et fidibus iuvat
  placare et vituli sanguine debito
custodes Numidae deos,
  qui nunc Hesperia sospes ab ultima

caris multa sodalibus,
  nulli plura tamen dividit oscula
quam dulci Lamiae, memor
  actae non alio rege puertiae

mutataeque simul togae.
  Cressa ne careat pulchra dies nota,
neu promptae modus amphorae,
  neu morem in Salium sit requies pedum,

neu multi Damalis meri
  Bassum Threïcia vincat amystide,
neu desint epulis rosae
  neu vivax apium neu breve lilium.

Omnes in Damalin putris
  deponent oculos, nec Damalis novo
divelletur adultero,
  lascivis hederis ambitiosior.

With dancing and with incense and with music
And offerings to the kindness of the gods
Who brought him safely home from farthest Spain

Let's welcome Numida back among his friends.
He is greeting and embracing all of them,
And most of all his old friend Lamia—

The two of them went to school to the same teacher,
And shared the rite of the toga change together.
Today's a red-letter day for all of us.

Numida has come home, break out the wine.
Let's let there be no letup in the dancing.
Let Bassus and fair Damalis compete

To show each other how to dance and drink.
Let there be lots of flowers, let there be roses,
Let there be lilies, and long-lived blossom-of-parsley,

Flowers that quickly fade and flowers that don't.
Though everyone longs for Damalis, Damalis clings
Like amorous ivy to Numida come home.

Nunc est bibendum, nunc pede libero
pulsanda tellus, nunc Saliaribus
  ornare pulvinar deorum
    tempus erat dapibus, sodales.

Antehac nefas depromere Caecubum
cellis avitis, dum Capitolio
  regina dementis ruinas,
    funus et imperio parabat

contaminato cum grege turpium
morbo virorum, quidlibet impotens
  sperare fortunaque dulci
    ebria. Sed minuit furorem

vix una sospes navis ab ignibus,
mentemque lymphatam Mareotico
  redegit in veros timores
    Caesar, ab Italia volantem

remis adurgens, accipiter velut
mollis columbas aut leporem citus
  venator in campis nivalis
    Haemoniae, daret ut catenis

fatale monstrum. Quae generosius
perire quaerens nec muliebriter
  expavit ensem nec latentis
    classe cita reparavit oras;

ausa et iacentem visere regiam
vultu sereno, fortis et asperas
  tractare serpentes, ut atrum
    corpore combiberet venenum,

deliberata morte ferocior;
saevis Liburnis scilicet invidens
  privata deduci superbo
    non humilis mulier triumpho.

At last the day has come for celebration,
For dancing and for drinking, bringing out
The couches with their images of gods
Adorned in preparation for the feast.

Before today it would have been wrong to call
For the festive Caecuban wine from the vintage bins,
It would have been wrong while that besotted queen,
With her vile gang of sick polluted creatures,

Crazed with hope and drunk with her past successes,
Was planning the death and destruction of the empire.
But, comrades, she came to and sobered up
When not one ship, almost, of all her fleet

Escaped unburned, and Caesar saw to it
That she was restored from madness to a state
Of realistic terror. The way a hawk
Chases a frightened dove or as a hunter

Chases a hare across the snowy steppes,
His galleys chased this fleeing queen, intending
To put the monster prodigy into chains
And bring her back to Rome. But she desired

A nobler fate than that; she did not seek
To hide her remnant fleet in a secret harbor;
Nor did she, like a woman, quail with fear
At the thought of what it is the dagger does.

She grew more fierce as she beheld her death.
Bravely, as if unmoved, she looked upon
The ruins of her palace; bravely reached out,
And touched the poison snakes, and picked them up,

And handled them, and held them to her so
Her heart might drink its fill of their black venom.
In truth—no abject woman she—she scorned
In triumph to be brought in galleys unqueened

Across the seas to Rome to be a show.

i.38

Persicos odi, puer, apparatus;
displicent nexae philyra coronae;
mitte sectari rosa quo locorum
    sera moretur.

Simplici myrto nihil allabores
sedulus curo: neque te ministrum
dedecet myrtus neque me sub arta
    vite bibentem.

I dislike elaborate show, as, for example,
"Persian" garlands too intricately woven,
So don't go looking everywhere for somewhere
Where the last rose blooming anywhere might be.

Don't bother to look for anything less simple
Than simple myrtle, suitable to the scene:
The garlanded cupbearer waiting, and garlanded I,
Here in the shade of the arbor, drinking my wine.

BOOK TWO

ii.1

Motum ex Metello consule civicum
bellique causas et vitia et modos
    ludumque Fortunae gravisque
        principum amicitias et arma

nondum expiatis uncta cruoribus,
periculosae plenum opus aleae,
    tractas et incedis per ignes
        suppositos cineri doloso.

Paulum severae Musa tragoediae
desit theatris; mox, ubi publicas
    res ordinaris, grande munus
        Cecropio repetes cothurno,

insigne maestis praesidium reis
et consulenti, Pollio, curiae,
    cui laurus aeternos honores
        Delmatico peperit triumpho.

Iam nunc minaci murmure cornuum
perstringis auris, iam litui strepunt,
    iam fulgor armorum fugacis
        terret equos equitumque vultus.

Audire magnos iam videor duces,
non indecoro pulvere sordidos,
    et cuncta terrarum subacta
        praeter atrocem animum Catonis.

Iuno et deorum quisquis amicior
Afris inulta cesserat impotens
    tellure victorum nepotes
        rettulit inferias Iugurthae.

Do not be absent long from the tragic stage,
Pollio, famous for this, and famous too

For your victory in Dalmatia, and for wise
Counsel in the councils of the Senate,

And for the defense of those accused in court.
Now you are setting out to tell the story

Of the civil wars that began so long ago,
In the consulship of Metellus: the ways they happened,

The reasons for the wars, the mistakes that were made,
The consequences of friendships of the great ones,

All the blood shed that to this day's unpaid for.
What you are undertaking is full of danger.

Fire is burning under the ashes you walk on.
Even now I seem to hear the raucous sound

Of the war horns in the music you create.
The deafening noise of trumpets fills my ear.

I see the javelins and swords, the shields,
The helmets, and the breastplates. I see the terror

In the terrified horses' faces, and I see
The terror in the faces of their riders.

I hear the exhortations of the captains
Covered with not inglorious filth; I see

The world brought down by Roman arms, in spite
Of Cato's virtuous stubbornness of heart.

Helpless to help, Juno and all the gods
Allied with her to favor Africa

Quis non Latino sanguine pinguior
campus sepulcris impia proelia
    testatur auditumque Medis
       Hesperiae sonitum ruinae?

Qui gurges aut quae flumina lugubris
ignara belli? Quod mare Dauniae
    non decoloravere caedes?
       Quae caret ora cruore nostro?

Sed ne relictis, Musa procax, iocis
Ceae retractes munera neniae,
    mecum Dionaeo sub antro
       quaere modos leviore plectro.

From Africa had withdrawn their help, and then
Renewed the offer with the sacrifice

Of the bodies of the grandsons of the victors,
As tribute to the African, Jugurtha.

What field is there that isn't fertilized
With Roman blood, where Roman graves bear witness

To the impiety of Romans fighting Romans?
Witness the noise of Hesperia's crashing fall,

Pleasing the ears of the Parthian enemy
Who heard it on the other side of the world.

What standing pool is there, what flowing river,
That doesn't know what Roman blood tastes like?

Where is it where the foam of breaking waves
Doesn't leave the stain of Roman blood on the sand?

My wayward Muse, find us a place to hide
From such a story and from such a music,

Some grotto or some cavern Venus-blessed,
Where I can play a lighter tune than this.

ii.2

Nullus argento color est avaris
abdito terris, inimice lamnae
Crispe Sallusti, nisi temperato
    splendeat usu.

Vivet extento Proculeius aevo,
notus in fratres animi paterni:
illum aget penna metuente solvi
    fama superstes.

Latius regnes avidum domando
spiritum, quam si Libyam remotis
Gadibus iungas et uterque Poenus
    serviat uni.

Crescit indulgens sibi dirus hydrops,
nec sitim pellit, nisi causa morbi
fugerit venis et aquosus albo
    corpore languor.

Redditum Cyri solio Phraäten
dissidens plebi numero beatorum
eximit Virtus populumque falsis
    dedocet uti

vocibus, regnum et diadema tutum
deferens uni propriamque laurum,
quisquis ingentis oculo irretorto
    spectat acervos.

That metal's dull that in the covetous earth
Is hidden away. You know that this is so,
Crispus Sallustius, because you know
How valueless is that which isn't polished
To brightest shining by intelligent use.
So Proculeius shines, known as he is

For constant fatherly kindness to his brothers;
His fame will bear him up on wings as constant.
The man who governs well his own heart governs
A wider kingdom than the man who governs
All there is from Libya over to Spain,
Bringing all Carthage under one single rule.

Unslaked, the dropsy, thirsty, wants still more
The more it's given to drink, thirsting for more,
And, drowsily, drinks still more, and thirsts, and drinks
Still more, unslaked, no end to this, unless
The cause be expelled entirely from the veins
Of the pale languorous waterlogged suffering body.

Ambitious Phraates is king of Cyprus again?
Virtue dissents from the crowd that calls *him* happy.
Virtue teaches the proper names of things,
Expelling the wrong. That man alone is happy
And wears his crown secure who can gaze untempted
At all the heaped-up treasure of the world.

ii.3

Aequam memento rebus in arduis
servare mentem, non secus in bonis
    ab insolenti temperatam
        laetitia, moriture Delli,

seu maestus omni tempore vixeris,
seu te in remoto gramine per dies
    festos reclinatum bearis
        interiore nota Falerni.

Quo pinus ingens albaque populus
umbram hospitalem consociare amant
    ramis? Quid obliquo laborat
        lympha fugax trepidare rivo?

Huc vina et unguenta et nimium brevis
flores amoenae ferre iube rosae,
    dum res et aetas et sororum
        fila trium patiuntur atra.

Cedes coëmptis saltibus et domo
villaque, flavus quam Tiberis lavit,
    cedes, et exstructis in altum
        divitiis potietur heres.

When things are bad, be steady in your mind;
    Dellius, don't be
Too unrestrainedly joyful in good fortune.
    You are going to die.

It doesn't matter at all whether you spend
    Your days and nights in sorrow,
Or, on the other hand, in holiday pleasure,
    Drinking Falernian wine

Of an excellent vintage year, on the river bank.
    Why is it, do you suppose,
That the dark branches of those tall pines and those
    Poplars' silvery leafy

Branches love to join, coming together,
    Creating a welcoming shade?
Haven't you noticed how in the quiet river
    The current shows signs of hurry,

Urging itself to go forward, going somewhere,
    Making its purposeful way?
By all means tell your servants to bring you wine,
    Perfumes, and the utterly lovely

Too briefly blossoming flowers of the villa garden;
    Yes, of course, while youth,
And circumstance, and the black threads of the Sisters
    Suffer this to be so.

You're going to have to yield those upland pastures,
    The ones you bought just lately;
You're going to yield the townhouse, and the villa,
    The country place whose margin

The Tiber washes as it moves along.
    Heirs will possess all that
Which you have gathered. It does not matter at all
    If you are rich, with kings

Divesne, prisco natus ab Inacho,
nil interest an pauper et infima
 de gente sub divo moreris;
  victima nil miserantis Orci.

Omnes eodem cogimur, omnium
versatur urna serius ocius
 sors exitura et nos in aeternum
  exsilium impositura cumbae.

Forefathers of your pride; no matter; or poor,
  Fatherless under the sky.
You will be sacrificed to Orcus without pity.
  All of us together

Are being gathered; the lot of each of us
  Is in the shaking urn
With all the other lots, and like the others
  Sooner or later our lot

Will fall out from the urn; and so we are chosen to take
  Our place in that dark boat,
In that dark boat, that bears us all away
  From here to where no one comes back from ever.

ii.4

Ne sit ancillae tibi amor pudori,
Xanthia Phoceu. Prius insolentem
serva Briseis niveo colore
    movit Achillem;

movit Aiacem Telamone natum
forma captivae dominum Tecmessae;
arsit Atrides medio in triumpho
    virgine rapta,

barbarae postquam cecidere turmae
Thessalo victore et ademptus Hector
tradidit fessis leviora tolli
    Pergama Graïs.

Nescias an te generum beati
Phyllidis flavae decorent parentes:
regium certe genus et penatis
    maeret iniquos.

Crede non illam tibi de scelesta
plebe dilectam neque sic fidelem,
sic lucro aversam potuisse nasci
    matre pudenda.

Bracchia et vultum teretisque suras
integer laudo; fuge suspicari,
cuius octavum trepidavit aetas
    claudere lustrum.

ii.4 / *To Xanthias*

Xanthias, don't be ashamed of falling in love
With a young woman who happens to be a slave.
Achilles, after all, was in love with Briseis;

And Ajax, the proud, the son of Telamon, fell
Head over heels for the beautiful captive Tecmessa;
And Atrides burned with love for a captive too—

This was exactly at the moment when,
Because of Achilles, Hector was lost to Troy,
And Troy the more easily fell to the weary Greeks.

How do you know that your blond Phyllis isn't
Descended from highborn parents? Why, she must
Have come down from *kings*! Surely your Phyllis grieves

Because the unkind gods have brought her down
From what she was to this her present station.
You can be sure of this: a person like her,

So without guile or greed, so faithful and selfless,
Must be the worthy child of a worthy mother.
—Nor should you be suspicious when I praise

The beauty of her face, her arms, her ankles.
Surely I must be free of your suspicion,
Since I have reached the age that I have reached.

ii.5

Nondum subacta ferre iugum valet
cervice, nondum munia comparis
    aequare nec tauri ruentis
        in venerem tolerare pondus.

Circa virentis est animus tuae
campos iuvencae, nunc fluviis gravem
    solantis aestum, nunc in udo
        ludere cum vitulis salicto

praegestientis. Tolle cupidinem
immitis uvae: iam tibi lividos
    distinguet Autumnus racemos
        purpureo varius colore.

Iam te sequetur (currit enim ferox
aetas, et illi quos tibi dempserit
    apponet annos), iam proterva
        fronte petet Lalage maritum,

dilecta quantum non Pholoë fugax,
non Chloris, albo sic umero nitens,
    ut pura nocturno renidet
        luna mari Cnidiusve Gyges,

quem si puellarum insereres choro,
mire sagacis falleret hospites
    discrimen obscurum solutis
        crinibus ambiguoque vultu.

ii.5 / *To a Suitor*

She isn't ready yet to bear the yoke
Submissively, not ready yet to bear
The weight and heat of an impassioned lover.

As yet her heart is given to the meadow
And the cool streams and to the willow groves,
With her companions sheltering from the heat

Of the summer sun. The fruit is still unripe.
It won't be long before the days of autumn
Darken to purple the clusters on the vine.

It won't be long, for so it goes with seasons,
Before it will be she who seeks you out,
Lalage forwardly looking for a mate,

Delighting you more than Pholoë did, the shy,
Or Chloris, whose shoulders are so beautiful,
White as the moonlight shining on the sea,

Or Cnidian Gyges, who, if you found him among
A company of maidens, you almost couldn't
Tell him from one of them, with his long hair

And his boy's face so exactly like a girl's face.

ii.6

Septimi, Gadis aditure mecum et
Cantabrum indoctum iuga ferre nostra et
barbaras Syrtis, ubi Maura semper
    aestuat unda,

Tibur Argeo positum colono
sit meae sedes utinam senectae,
sit modus lasso maris et viarum
    militiaeque.

Unde si Parcae prohibent iniquae,
dulce pellitis ovibus Galaesi
flumen et regnata petam Laconi
    rura Phalantho.

Ille terrarum mihi praeter omnis
angulus ridet, ubi non Hymetto
mella decedunt viridique certat
    baca Venafro;

ver ubi longum tepidasque praebet
Iuppiter brumas, et amicus Aulon
fertili Baccho minimum Falernis
    invidet uvis.

Septimius, I know
  That you are ready to go
Along with me to the ends
  Of the earth on whatever journey
And to whatever place,
  Whether it be Cádiz
By the Gates of Hercules,
  Or that wild mountainous land
Whose people have not yet learned
  To bear our Roman rule,
Or over the sea to barbarous
  Sidra where the waves,
Unsettled, heave along
  The Mauritanian shore.

Let Tivoli be the place
  To which I come to spend
My old age in when I
  Grow tired of wars, and seas,
And wandering over them.
  But if the unkind Fates
Deny that this can be,
  Then I will seek the land
Where the Galeasus River
  Flows and where the sheep
Wear skins so as to protect
  Their perfect curly wool;
That part of the world whose honey
  Is just as good as that
Honey from Hymettus
  So famous for being good;
And its olives are the equal
  Of the olives of Venafrum;
And the vineyards there at Aulon
  (Since Bacchus loves them so)
Have no reason to envy
  The vineyards of Falernum.

Ille te mecum locus et beatae
postulant arces; ibi tu calentem
debita sparges lacrima favillam
vatis amici.

This is the place where Jove
  Kindly permits the spring
To last for a long time
  And kindly permits the winter
To be as mild as can be.
  Septimius, Tarentum
And the blessed hills around it,
  The countryside of my childhood,
Summon you and me.
  There someday you will mourn
At the grave of him who was
  A poet, and your friend.

ii.7

O saepe mecum tempus in ultimum
deducte Bruto militiae duce,
   quis te redonavit Quiritem
     dis patriis Italoque caelo,

Pompei, meorum prime sodalium,
cum quo morantem saepe diem mero
   fregi, coronatus nitentis
     malobathro Syrio capillos?

Tecum Philippos et celerem fugam
sensi relicta non bene parmula,
   cum fracta virtus et minaces
     turpe solum tetigere mento.

Sed me per hostis Mercurius celer
denso paventem sustulit aëre;
   te rursus in bellum resorbens
     unda fretis tulit aestuosis.

Ergo obligatam redde Iovi dapem,
longaque fessum militia latus
   depone sub lauru mea nec
     parce cadis tibi destinatis.

Oblivioso levia Massico
ciboria exple, funde capacibus
   unguenta de conchis. Quis udo
     deproperare apio coronas

curatve myrto? Quem Venus arbitrum
dicet bibendi? Non ego sanius
   bacchabor Edonis; recepto
     dulce mihi furere est amico.

ii.7 / *To an Old Comrade in the Army of Brutus*

Dear friend who fought so often, together with me,
In the ranks of Brutus in hardship and in danger,
Under whose sponsorship have you come back,
A citizen again, beneath our sky?

Pompey, we drank together so many times,
And we were together in the Philippi fight,
The day I ran away, leaving my shield,
And Mercury got me out of it, carrying me

In a cloud, in a panic, right through the enemy rage;
But the undertow of a wave carried you back
Into the boiling waters of the war.
Come, stretch your weary legs out under this tree;

Let's dedicate a feast to Jupiter
Just as we told each other we'd do someday.
I've got good food to eat, good wine to drink;
Come celebrate old friendship under the laurel.

ii.8

Ulla si iuris tibi peierati
poena, Barine, nocuisset umquam,
dente si nigro fieres vel uno
    turpior ungui,

crederem. Sed tu simul obligasti
perfidum votis caput, enitescis
pulchrior multo iuvenumque prodis
    publica cura.

Expedit matris cineres opertos
fallere et toto taciturna noctis
signa cum caelo gelidaque divos
    morte carentis.

Ridet hoc, inquam, Venus ipsa; rident
simplices Nymphae ferus et Cupido,
semper ardentis acuens sagittas
    cote cruenta.

Adde quod pubes tibi crescit omnis,
servitus crescit nova, nec priores
impiae tectum dominae relinquunt,
    saepe minati.

Te suis matres metuunt iuvencis,
te senes parci miseraeque nuper
virgines nuptae, tua ne retardet
    aura maritos.

ii.8 / To Barina

Barina, if by a single sign, let's say
  By a blackened nail or a discolored tooth,
You showed that you had been punished even a little
  For the lies you told and for the vows you broke,

Then I would have reason to trust you now, but no,
  No sooner have you broken a solemn vow
Or told a lie, than you shine forth, a star,
  More beautiful than you ever were before.

Everyone marvels. So if it suits you to swear
  By the ashes of your mother in the tomb,
You will, or by the taciturn witnessing stars,
  Or by the gods immune to the cold of death.

Venus herself is amused by this, and laughs,
  And so do her maidens, and so does Cupid too,
Busily sharpening up his cruel darts
  On a whetstone stained with the blood of the hearts of lovers.

A whole new generation of young men
  Is growing up only to be a fresh
Supply of Barina's slaves, and the older crowd,
  Though swearing to leave you, cannot possibly do so.

You terrify mothers terrified for their sons,
  And fathers terrified for their sons' money,
And young brides terrified lest their young husbands never
  Come home tonight, spellbound in your power.

ii.9

Non semper imbres nubibus hispidos
manant in agros aut mare Caspium
    vexant inaequales procellae
        usque, nec Armeniis in oris,

amice Valgi, stat glacies iners
menses per omnis, aut Aquilonibus
    querqueta Gargani laborant
        et foliis viduantur orni:

tu semper urges flebilibus modis
Mysten ademptum, nec tibi Vespero
    surgente decedunt amores
        nec rapidum fugiente solem.

At non ter aevo functus amabilem
ploravit omnis Antilochum senex
    annos, nec impubem parentes
        Troïlon aut Phrygiae sorores

flevere semper. Desine mollium
tandem querellarum, et potius nova
    cantemus Augusti tropaea
        Caesaris, et rigidum Niphaten,

Medumque flumen gentibus additum
victis minores volvere vertices,
    intraque praescriptum Gelonos
        exiguis equitare campis.

ii.9 / *To Valgius*

Rain doesn't fall on rain-soaked fields forever,
Nor, Valgius, dear friend, do the winds stir up
The Caspian unceasingly, nor does
The winter ice stay frozen all year round

In icy Armenia, nor do North Wind gales
Unendingly batter and sway the oak-tree groves
And strip the shivering ash-trees of their leaves
On stormy Mount Gargano Promontory.

But, Valgius, dear friend, your grieving for
Your own beloved Mystes goes on regardless
Of the rising of the evening star called Vesper
And regardless of the sun when at its rising

Vesper is sent away. Nestor, you know,
Who lived so many years, didn't go on weeping
Forever for his son Antilochus,
And Troilus's parents and his sisters

At last dried up their tears. Dry up your tears,
And let us sing instead about the trophies
Caesar has lately added to the list:
Rocky Niphates now belongs to Rome,

And, now that the Medes are conquered, the Euphrates
River flows in fetters, and the far-off
Gelonian bowmen now can ride and raid
Only within the borders Rome prescribes.

Rectius vives, Licini, neque altum
semper urgendo neque, dum procellas
cautus horrescis, nimium premendo
    litus iniquum.

Auream quisquis mediocritatem
diligit, tutus caret obsoleti
sordibus tecti, caret invidenda
    sobrius aula.

Saepius ventis agitatur ingens
pinus et celsae graviore casu
decidunt turres feriuntque summos
    fulgura montis.

Sperat infestis, metuit secundis
alteram sortem bene praeparatum
pectus. Informis hiemes reducit
    Iuppiter; idem

summovet. Non, si male nunc, et olim
sic erit: quondam cithara tacentem
suscitat Musam neque semper arcum
    tendit Apollo.

Rebus angustis animosus atque
fortis appare; sapienter idem
contrahes vento nimium secundo
    turgida vela.

You'll do better, Licinius, not to spend your life
Venturing too far out on the dangerous waters,
Or else, for fear of storms, staying too close in
To the dangerous rocky shoreline. That man does best
Who chooses the middle way, so he doesn't end up
Living under a roof that's going to ruin
Or in some gorgeous mansion everyone envies.
The tallest pine shakes most in a wind storm;
The loftiest tower falls down with the loudest crash;
The lightning bolt heads straight for the mountain top.
Always expect reversals: be hopeful in trouble,
Be worried when things go well. That's how it is
For the man whose heart is ready for anything.
It's true that Jupiter brings on the hard winters;
It's also true that Jupiter takes them away.
If things are bad right now, they won't always be.
Apollo isn't always drawing his bow;
There are times when he takes up his lyre and plays,
And awakens the music sleeping upon the strings.
Be resolute when things are going against you,
But shorten sail when the fair wind blows too strong.

Quid bellicosus Cantaber et Scythes,
Hirpine Quincti, cogitet Hadria
   divisus obiecto, remittas
      quaerere, nec trepides in usum

poscentis aevi pauca. Fugit retro
levis iuventas et decor, arida
   pellente lascivos amores
      canitie facilemque somnum.

Non semper idem floribus est honor
vernis, neque uno luna rubens nitet
   vultu. Quid aeternis minorem
      consiliis animum fatigas?

Cur non sub alta vel platano vel hac
pinu iacentes sic temere et rosa
   canos odorati capillos,
      dum licet, Assyriaque nardo

potamus uncti? Dissipat Euhius
curas edacis. Quis puer ocius
   restinguet ardentis Falerni
      pocula praetereunte lympha?

Quis devium scortum eliciet domo
Lyden? Eburna dic, age, cum lyra
   maturet, in comptum Lacaenae
      more comas religata nodum.

ii.11 / *To Quinctius Hirpinus*

Don't worry so much about whatever it is
The Cantabrians in Iberia might be planning,
Or the war-loving Scythians on the other side
Of the Adriatic. Life's too short for that.

Youth and good looks go by pretty fast, after all,
And we go on getting older. The pleasures of sex
Get to be less and less than they used to be;
And easy sleep's no longer so easily come by.

Flowers don't bloom forever; and as for the moon,
It never stays the same. The brightness dims.
Why weary yourself staring into the dark,
Trying to see what eyes are unable to see?

Let's have a drink, under the olive trees.
Bacchus helps out. Where is the servant to send
To fetch some brook water to water this wine a little?
Who'll go looking for Lyde? Persuade her to come

With her ivory lyre to sing and play us some music,
Here, under the trees. Beautiful Lyde,
With her hair arranged as in the Laconian fashion,
Pinned up behind in an elegant simple knot.

ii.12

Nolis longa ferae bella Numantiae
nec durum Hannibalem nec Siculum mare
Poeno purpureum sanguine mollibus
    aptari citharae modis,

nec saevos Lapithas et nimium mero
Hylaeum domitosque Herculea manu
Telluris iuvenes, unde periculum
    fulgens contremuit domus

Saturni veteris; tuque pedestribus
dices historiis proelia Caesaris,
Maecenas, melius ductaque per vias
    regum colla minacium.

Me dulcis dominae Musa Licymniae
cantus, me voluit dicere lucidum
fulgentis oculos et bene mutuis
    fidum pectus amoribus;

quam nec ferre pedem dedecuit choris
nec certare ioco nec dare bracchia
ludentem nitidis virginibus sacro
    Dianae celebris die.

Num tu quae tenuit dives Achaemenes
aut pinguis Phrygiae Mygdonias opes
permutare velis crine Licymniae,
    plenas aut Arabum domos,

cum flagrantia detorquet ad oscula
cervicem, aut facili saevitia negat,
quae poscente magis gaudeat eripi,
    interdum rapere occupet?

You wouldn't want to have to sit and listen
To the soft voice of the cithara telling you stories
About the long wars against the fearsome Spaniards,
Or Hannibal the tough, or how the sea

Near Sicily ran red with Punic blood,
Or about the Lapiths and the wine-crazed Centaurs,
Or how by the punishing hand of Hercules
The Sons of the Earth were tamed, the Giants who caused

Old Saturn's shining house to quake with fear.
Maecenas, you'd be better able to tell
Straightforwardly in prose stories like these,
About the triumphs of Caesar and about how

Chained by the neck once-dangerous kings paraded
Disgraced along the streets of jubilant Rome.
Instead of this the Muse wants me to use
The peaceable music of my cithara

To celebrate Lycymnia's shining eyes,
Lycymnia's wit, Lycymnia's lovely singing,
Lycymnia's faithful loving marital heart,
Lycymnia dancing with such seemly grace,

Lycymnia joining hands with the festal band
Of maidens on Diana's sacred day.
You wouldn't trade a single lock of hair
From your Lycymnia's head for all the wealth

Of Persian Achaemenes, nor all the riches
Of Arabia, nor all that Minos owned,
As Lycymnia bends her neck to accept your kisses
Or with mock severity refuses them.

Ille et nefasto te posuit die,
quicumque primum, et sacrilega manu
   produxit, arbos, in nepotum
      perniciem opprobriumque pagi.

Illum et parentis crediderim sui
fregisse cervicem et penetralia
   sparsisse nocturno cruore
      hospitis; ille venena Colcha

et quicquid usquam concipitur nefas
tractavit, agro qui statuit meo
   te, triste lignum, te caducum
      in domini caput immerentis.

Quid quisque vitet, numquam homini satis
cautum est in horas. Navita Bosphorum
   Poenus perhorrescit neque ultra
      caeca timet aliunde fata;

miles sagittas et celerem fugam
Parthi, catenas Parthus et Italum
   robur; sed improvisa leti
      vis rapuit rapietque gentis.

Quam paene furvae regna Proserpinae
et iudicantem vidimus Aeacum
   sedesque discriptas piorum et
      Aeoliis fidibus querentem

Sappho puellis de popularibus
et te sonantem plenius aureo,
   Alcaee, plectro dura navis,
      dura fugae mala, dura belli.

Utrumque sacro digna silentio
mirantur umbrae dicere; sed magis
   pugnas et exactos tyrannos
      densum umeris bibit aure vulgus.

Whoever it may have been who planted you,
He chose an unholy day to do it on,
And nurtured you profanely with intent
Against the future and to disgrace this valley.

That man probably strangled his own father;
His hearth is probably stained with the blood of a houseguest
He murdered at midnight; he's probably expert at poison
Or any other crime you choose to name—

That man who planted you you wretched rotten
Falling tree come down on your master's head.
Nobody watches out for what he should
Watch out for. Thus, the Phoenician sailor is scared

Of the Bosporus, but he isn't scared of the fate
That lies beyond. The Roman soldier is scared
Of the Parthian's arrows; the Parthian's scared of the Roman.
But that which will take them away can't be foreseen.

How close I came to being brought down to see
The house of dark Persephone and to see
The chair that Aeacus sits on making his judgment,
And to see the place down there set apart for the just.

How close I came to hearing the music of Sappho
Complaining of those young women of her island,
And the ampler music of Alcaeus as
With a golden plectrum he plucks the strings and tells

Of the hardships of voyage, the hardships of exile, and war.
The shades down there gather together to hear
The music of Alcaeus and of Sappho.
Hushed, they wonder at both, but most of all,

Shoulder to ghostly shoulder thronging they listen
To stories of battle and tyrants expelled from their thrones.
The many-headed monster Cerberus listens,
His black ears lowered to hear Alcaeus' music;

Quid mirum, ubi illis carminibus stupens
demittit atras belua centiceps
   auris, et intorti capillis
      Eumenidum recreantur angues?

Quin et Prometheus et Pelopis parens
dulci laborem decipitur sono,
   nec curat Orion leones
      aut timidos agitare lyncas.

The snakes in the hair of the Furies pause in their writhing;
Prometheus and Tantalus suspend
Their suffering for a while; Orion the hunter
Ceases to chase the lion and timid lynx.

Eheu fugaces, Postume, Postume,
labuntur anni, nec pietas moram
    rugis et instanti senectae
      adferet indomitaeque morti;

non, si trecenis, quotquot eunt dies,
amice, places illacrimabilem
    Plutona tauris, qui ter amplum
      Geryonen Tityonque tristi

compescit unda—scilicet omnibus,
quicumque terrae munere vescimur,
    enaviganda, sive reges
      sive inopes erimus coloni.

Frustra cruento Marte carebimus
fractisque rauci fluctibus Hadriae,
    frustra per autumnos nocentem
      corporibus metuemus Austrum.

Visendus ater flumine languido
Cocytos errans et Danaï genus
    infame damnatusque longi
      Sisyphus Aeolides laboris.

Linquenda tellus et domus et placens
uxor, neque harum quas colis arborum
    te praeter invisas cupressos
      ulla brevem dominum sequetur.

Absumet heres Caecuba dignior
servata centum clavibus et mero
    tinguet pavimentum superbo
      pontificum potiore cenis.

How the years go by, alas how the years go by.
Behaving well can do nothing at all about it.
Wrinkles will come, old age will come, and death,
Indomitable. Nothing at all will work.

Offer in pledge three hundred oxen a day,
Unweeping Pluto will never be appeased.
Giants he holds in thrall down there for ever
On the other bank of that dark stream that all

Who eat and drink the good things of the earth
Must cross at last, whoever they may be,
Rich man or poor man, whatever, it doesn't matter.
In vain that you fear what's borne on the sick South Wind.

In vain that you survived the bloody field.
In vain that you made for port having ridden out
The terrible storm that time on the Adriatic.
It doesn't matter at all. However it happens,

Each one of us shall come to see the black
River Cocytos wandering through the region
Where Danaus' wicked daughters endlessly suffer
And Sisyphus for ever labors on.

Each one of us must leave the earth he loves
And leave his home and leave his tender wife,
And leave the trees he planted and took good care of.
Only the cypress grows along those banks.

Your heir will drink the choice Caecuban wine
You did not know that you were saving for him
When you locked it up securely in your cellar.
The wine he spills is priceless, it doesn't matter.

ii.15

Iam pauca aratro iugera regiae
moles relinquent, undique latius
   extenta visentur Lucrino
      stagna lacu, platanusque caelebs

evincet ulmos; tum violaria et
myrtus et omnis copia narium
   spargent olivetis odorem
      fertilibus domino priori.

Tum spissa ramis laurea fervidos
excludet ictus. Non ita Romuli
   praescriptum et intonsi Catonis
      auspiciis veterumque norma.

Privatus illis census erat brevis,
commune magnum; nulla decempedis
   metata privatis opacam
      porticus excipiebat Arcton,

nec fortuitum spernere caespitem
leges sinebant, oppida publico
   sumptu iubentes et deorum
      templa novo decorare saxo.

It won't be long before the little farms
Will be crowded out of being by the great
Estates of these latter days with their enormous
Fish ponds bigger than Lake Lucrinus is.

Now the old elm is yielding to the new
Plane tree (to which no vine will ever cling)
And the ubiquitous fragrance of the myrtle,
The violets, and the other sweet-smelling flowers,

Scatters itself and spreads throughout the groves
Of ancient olive trees which once rewarded
Their owners' patient labor. And pretty soon
The decorative laurel tree will quite shut out

The hot sun's rays once needed by the farmer.
It wasn't like this at all in Cato's time
Or Romulus's time. Our fathers' ways
Were not these ways. Nobody minded then

That his holding was nothing more than a little farm.
They thought more then about the common good.
Nobody had a great big portico then,
Built on the north for shade from the summer sun.

Brick houses roofed with thatch were common as dirt
And nobody scorned them. The law, however, required
That everyone should pay his share of the cost
Of adorning with marble the temples of the gods.

ii.16

Otium divos rogat in patenti
prensus Aegaeo, simul atra nubes
condidit lunam neque certa fulgent
    sidera nautis;

otium bello furiosa Thrace,
otium Medi pharetra decori,
Grosphe, non gemmis neque purpura ve-
    nale nec auro.

Non enim gazae neque consularis
summovet lictor miseros tumultus
mentis et curas laqueata circum
    tecta volantis.

Vivitur parvo bene, cui paternum
splendet in mensa tenui salinum
nec levis somnos timor aut cupido
    sordidus aufert.

Quid brevi fortes iaculamur aevo
multa? Quid terras alio calentis
sole mutamus? Patriae quis exsul
    se quoque fugit?

Scandit aeratas vitiosa navis
Cura nec turmas equitum relinquit,
ocior cervis et agente nimbos
    ocior Euro.

Laetus in praesens animus quod ultra est
oderit curare et amara lento
temperet risu. Nihil est ab omni
    parte beatum.

Abstulit clarum cita mors Achillem,
longa Tithonum minuit senectus;
et mihi forsan, tibi quod negarit,
    porriget hora.

The sailor out on the sea, a storm coming on,
When the black clouds hide away the light of the moon
And there's no light of the stars to be guided by,
    Prays for calm weather.

The bellicose Thracian sometimes prays for a respite;
So does the warlike Mede with his ornate dagger;
But neither gold nor jewels nor rich dye-stuffs
    Can purchase peace. Peace isn't

Something money or some high office can buy.
They won't dispel the miseries the soul
Is vulnerable to, the anxieties that hover
    Around your coffered ceiling.

That man lives well who lives a frugal life.
On his table gleams the lovingly polished salt-dish
His father left him. Neither fear nor greed
    Disturbs his good night's sleep.

Why do we try so hard to own so much?
Why go south in the winter to find the sun?
Who ever went away to a foreign country
    And got away from himself?

Care scrambles aboard the rich man's brass-trimmed yacht;
Outruns the swiftest horses; outruns the deer;
Is swifter than Eurus, the squall-wind, driving the clouds,
    Raising a sudden storm.

Let the heart rejoice in whatever it has right now;
Don't worry about whatever might come in the future;
Turn it aside with a smile. There's no such thing
    As absolute guaranteed bliss.

Achilles in his glory was taken away;
Tithonus got old but look what he wasted away to;
And what the next minute might take away from you,
    It might offer instead to me.

Te greges centum Siculaeque circum
mugiunt vaccae, tibi tollit hinnitum
apta quadrigis equa, te bis Afro
    murice tinctae

vestiunt lanae; mihi parva rura et
spiritum Graiae tenuem Camenae
Parca non mendax dedit et malignum
    spernere vulgus.

Around your great farm house you can hear the lowing
Of your many herds of fine Sicilian cattle;
Your fine race-mare is whinnying in your stable;
   You wear the finest garments

Double-dyed with African purple dye.
To me the Fates have given a little house,
And a certain talent for rendering Grecian verses,
   And scorn for the envious.

Cur me querelis exanimas tuis?
Nec dis amicum est nec mihi te prius
   obire, Maecenas, mearum
      grande decus columenque rerum.

A, te meae si partem animae rapit
maturior vis, quid moror altera,
   nec carus aeque nec superstes
      integer? Ille dies utramque

ducet ruinam. Non ego perfidum
dixi sacramentum: ibimus, ibimus,
   utcumque praecedes, supremum
      carpere iter comites parati.

Me nec Chimaerae spiritus igneae
nec, si resurgat, centimanus Gyas
   divellet umquam: sic potenti
      Iustitiae placitumque Parcis.

Seu Libra seu me Scorpios adspicit
formidulosus, pars violentior
   natalis horae, seu tyrannus
      Hesperiae Capricornus undae,

Why do you weary me so
  With your anxieties?
Neither the gods nor I
  Desire that you should go
Before me into death.
  Your friendship is the thing
My life most glories in.
  It is what most sustains me.

Ah, if some unexpected
  Event should happen one day,
And carry you off who are
  The half of what I am,
What would the other half do,
  Going on living, neither
As dear as it used to be,
  Nor able to be by itself?

That fatal day would be
  The ruin of us both.
This oath is not sworn falsely:
  You and I will go together,
We will go together, Maecenas,
  I following your lead,
Whenever that day comes,
  Companions ready to go.

Neither the fiery breath
  Of the Chimera nor
The hundred hands of Gyas,
  The Giant, rising up
To keep me from being with you
  Could ever possibly do so.
It is the will of the right
  Nature of things, and it is

The will of the sister Fates
  That this is the way it should be.
I don't know whether it's Libra,

utrumque nostrum incredibili modo
consentit astrum. Te Iovis impio
   tutela Saturno refulgens
      eripuit volucrisque Fati

tardavit alas, cum populus frequens
laetum theatris ter crepuit sonum;
   me truncus illapsus cerebro
      sustulerat, nisi Faunus ictum

dextra levasset, Mercurialium
custos virorum. Reddere victimas
   aedemque votivam memento;
      nos humilem feriemus agnam.

Or Scorpio the dread,
Or Capricorn the goat,
The tyrant of the West,
Who dominates my chart,
But it is wonderful that

Our stars agree together
In such mutual consent.
The shining of the protector
Jupiter outshone
The evil light of Saturn
And stayed the hand of death,
On the happy day when you

Came back to the public counsels
And the glad applause broke out
In the Theater three times;
And Faunus, who is protector
Of poets, saw to it that
The falling tree that might
Have struck me dead did not.
We must sacrifice to the gods.

ii.18

Non ebur neque aureum
　mea renidet in domo lacunar,
non trabes Hymettiae
　premunt columnas ultima recisas
Africa, neque Attali
　ignotus heres regiam occupavi,
nec Laconicas mihi
　trahunt honestae purpuras clientae.
At fides et ingeni
　benigna vena est, pauperemque dives
me petit: nihil supra
　deos lacesso nec potentem amicum
largiora flagito,
　satis beatus unicis Sabinis.
Truditur dies die,
　novaeque pergunt interire lunae.
Tu secanda marmora
　locas sub ipsum funus et sepulcri
immemor struis domos,
　marisque Baïs obstrepentis urges
summovere litora,
　parum locuples continente ripa.
Quid quod usque proximos
　revellis agri terminos et ultra
limites clientium
　salis avarus? Pellitur paternos
in sinu ferens deos
　et uxor et vir sordidosque natos.
Nulla certior tamen
　rapacis Orci fine destinata
aula divitem manet
　erum. Quid ultra tendis? Aequa tellus
pauperi recluditur
　regumque pueris, nec satelles Orci
callidum Prometheä
　revexit auro captus. Hic superbum
Tantalum atque Tantali
　genus coërcet, hic levare functum
pauperem laboribus
　vocatus atque non vocatus audit.

ii.18 / *Greed*

You won't find ivory-decorated panels
Nor gilded either, in my house, nor crossbeams
Made out of marble from Greece, supported by columns

Made out of wood imported from Africa;
I haven't been left a fortune and a palace,
Nor in Laconia do they spin and dye

Elegant dresses I've ordered for elegant women.
But I have good faith and a genial sort of talent,
And, poor as I am, rich men seek me out.

I ask no more of the gods nor of my friend.
Day treads on day, moons wane, one after the other,
And you, on the edge of the grave, in the shadow of death,

Order up marble slabs to build a new palace
Out over the sounding waters of Baiae Bay,
Not satisfied with your land-bound opulence.

And what is more, you knock down the boundary markers
And encroach on the land next door that your tenant lives on,
And man and wife are driven out of their home,

Carrying in their arms their household gods
And their ill-clad children. But nothing is more sure
Than that the hall that waits for the rich man is

The palace of Orcus greedy to take him in.
Why always want more and more of whatever there is?
Earth opens up to offer her gifts to the rich

And to the poor, alike. Orcus's agent
Couldn't be bribed to carry Prometheus back,
Clever Prometheus, over the fatal river;

Proud Tantalus is in prison down there forever,
And Tantalus' son, forever and forever;
And Orcus hears, whether called or not, and comes

To liberate the poor man from his labor.

ii.19

Bacchum in remotis carmina rupibus
vidi docentem—credite posteri—
    Nymphasque discentis et auris
        capripedum Satyrorum acutas.

Euhoe, recenti mens trepidat metu,
plenoque Bacchi pectore turbidum
    laetatur. Euhoe, parce, Liber,
        parce, gravi metuende thyrso!

Fas pervicacis est mihi Thyiadas
vinique fontem lactis et uberes
    cantare rivos atque truncis
        lapsa cavis iterare mella;

fas et beatae coniugis additum
stellis honorem tectaque Penthei
    disiecta non leni ruina
        Thracis et exitium Lycurgi.

Tu flectis amnis, tu mare barbarum,
tu separatis uvidus in iugis
    nodo coërces viperino
        Bistonidum sine fraude crinis.

Tu, cum parentis regna per arduum
cohors Gigantum scanderet impia,
    Rhoetum retorsisti leonis
        unguibus horribilique mala;

quamquam choreïs aptior et iocis
ludoque dictus non sat idoneus
    pugnae ferebaris; sed idem
        pacis eras mediusque belli.

Te vidit insons Cerberus aureo
cornu decorum, leniter atterens
    caudam, et recedentis trilingui
        ore pedes tetigitque crura.

It was over there, on a ledge of that farther mountain,
Believe me, O those of you who descend from me,
I truly saw him there, on the ledge of that mountain,
Bacchus himself, I witnessed him, teaching his songs

To the listening nymphs and pointed-eared goat-footed satyrs!
My god, I'm still afraid, my heart is bursting,
Filled as I am with joy, filled with the god!
O Liber, spare me thy rod, O Bacchus, spare me!

It's fitting that I should sing and sing again
About the mad Bacchantes and the honey
Oozing from the hollow trunks of trees,
The streams of milk, and fountains of wine overflowing.

It's fitting that I should tell and retell the stories
Of the crowning of Ariadne among the stars,
And how the house of Pentheus fell down,
And the death of mad Lycurgus, too, in Thrace.

You rule the barbarous seas and divert the streams
Just as you wish. On far-off mountain peaks,
Florid with wine you bind the Maenads' hair
With fillets made of writhing serpents tied.

It was you who when the usurper gang of Giants
Came up the sky against your father Jove,
Your lion teeth and horrifying claws
Threw back Rhoetus down the sky again.

It has been said that Bacchus is more suited
To mirth and dance and play than he is to war,
But he has shown his jubilant power as well
In battle as he has in festival.

When he came down to Hades, and Cerberus first
Saw him, radiant, wearing his golden horns,
Cerberus' welcoming tail brushed Hades' floor;
When Bacchus left the place to return above

Triple-tongued Cerberus gently licked his feet.

ii.20

Non usitata nec tenui ferar
penna biformis per liquidum aethera
    vates, neque in terris morabor
        longius invidiaque maior

urbes relinquam. Non ego, pauperum
sanguis parentum, non ego, quem vocas,
    dilecte Maecenas, obibo
        nec Stygia cohibebor unda.

Iam iam residunt cruribus asperae
pelles, et album mutor in alitem
    superne, nascunturque leves
        per digitos umerosque plumae.

Iam Daedaleo notior Icaro
visam gementis litora Bosphori
    Syrtisque Gaetulas canorus
        ales Hyperboreosque campos.

Me Colchus et, qui dissimulat metum
Marsae cohortis, Dacus et ultimi
    noscent Geloni, me peritus
        discet Hiber Rhodanique potor.

Absint inani funere neniae
luctusque turpes et querimoniae;
    compesce clamorem ac sepulcri
        mitte supervacuos honores.

Biform, being a bard and being a bird,
I'll take my flight up through the brilliant air

On powerful wings, taking my leave of the city,
Taking my leave of envy, flying high.

Dearest Maecenas, I declare that I,
To whom you call, I, child of a former slave,

Will never die; that I will never be
Imprisoned by the waters of the Styx.

Even as I speak I feel the skin begin
To loosen, pucker, and wrinkle about my ankles;

I feel the feathers softly gather upon
My shoulders and my arms, becoming wings.

Melodious bird I'll fly above the moaning
Bosporus, more glorious than Icarus,

I'll coast along above the coast of Sidra
And over the fabled Hyperborean steppes.

The Colchians will hear, the Dacians too,
Who say they have no fear of Roman arms,

And farther still the Gelonians will listen,
The Iberians by the Ebro they will listen,

And those who drink the waters of the Rhone
Will learn to be more learnèd from my song.

Therefore when you in error think I've died,
Provide no ritual dirge, no eulogies,

No grievers weeping noisily at my tomb.
It's all superfluous, I won't be there.

BOOK THREE

Odi profanum vulgus et arceo;
favete linguis. Carmina non prius
   audita Musarum sacerdos
     virginibus puerisque canto.

Regum timendorum in proprios greges,
reges in ipsos imperium est Iovis,
   clari Giganteo triumpho,
     cuncta supercilio moventis.

Est ut viro vir latius ordinet
arbusta sulcis, hic generosior
   descendat in Campum petitor,
     moribus hic meliorque fama

contendat, illi turba clientium
sit maior: aequa lege Necessitas
   sortitur insignis et imos,
     omne capax movet urna nomen.

Destrictus ensis cui super impia
cervice pendet, non Siculae dapes
   dulcem elaborabunt saporem,
     non avium citharaeque cantus

somnum reducent. Somnus agrestium
lenis virorum non humilis domos
   fastidit umbrosamque ripam,
     non Zephyris agitata Tempe.

Desiderantem quod satis est neque
tumultuosum sollicitat mare
   nec saevus Arcturi cadentis
     impetus aut orientis Haedi,

non verberatae grandine vineae
fundusque mendax, arbore nunc aquas
   culpante, nunc torrentia agros
     sidera, nunc hiemes iniquas.

iii.1 / *Ostentation*

I scorn the profane crowd and therefore I
  Forbid them to come near. Be reverently
    Silent. The songs that I,
Priest of the Muses, sing, not sung before,
  I sing for the young alone.

Surely tremendous kings govern their own;
  And Jove, who conquered the Giants, governs the kings;
    All things obey his nod.

One man has holdings richer than another's,
  One comes to office favored by his birth,
Another by acclaim for what he has done,
  Another still by the crowds' unthinking applause.
    Necessity makes the choice.
No matter what your station or situation,
  Your name is shaken in the urn.

Damocles at the King of Sicily's feast,
  Above whose bended head
    The hovering sword
  Hangs by a single thread,
Will not enjoy the feast, nor will the songs
  Of caged songbirds nor music of the lyre
    Lull him to sleep again.
But sleep comes easily to the innocent house
  Of the simple peasant and to the shady banks
Of country streams and to the Vale of Tempe
  Where soft breezes wander.

And he for whom enough is enough will never
    Be troubled by raging sea
Nor by bad weather that comes when Arcturus falls
    Or when the Kid arises,
Neither when hailstorms batter down his vines
  Nor when his trees complain of torrential rains
    Or blasts of torrid Dog Star heat,
      Or evil wintry cold.

Contracta pisces aequora sentiunt
iactis in altum molibus; huc frequens
   caementa demittit redemptor
      cum famulis dominusque terrae

fastidiosus. Sed Timor et Minae
scandunt eodem quo dominus, neque
   decedit aerata triremi et
      post equitem sedet atra Cura.

Quod si dolentem nec Phrygius lapis
nec purpurarum sidere clarior
   delenit usus nec Falerna
      vitis Achaemeniumque costum,

cur invidendis postibus et novo
sublime ritu moliar atrium?
   Cur valle permutem Sabina
      divitias operosiores?

The startled fish in their waters know when the builder
  Displaces their placid waters with the rubble
Put down into the depths, on which to build
  A lofty seaside palace out over the waters
    For the proud owner for whom
Not even his land is enough. But Menace and Fear
  Are there in the seaside palace;
Anxiety is on board the elegant yacht,
  For all its trimmings of brass; black Sorrow sits
Behind the horseman as he rides his horse.

If neither purple silks, more lustrous than starlight,
  Nor Phrygian lapis, nor Falernian wine,
    Nor unguents from the East,
Can obliterate care, then why should I exchange
  My Sabine farm for an ostentatious house,
    The cause of envy in others?

Angustam amice pauperiem pati
robustus acri militia puer
  condiscat et Parthos ferocis
    vexet eques metuendus hasta,

vitamque sub divo et trepidis agat
in rebus. Illum ex moenibus hosticis
  matrona bellantis tyranni
    prospiciens et adulta virgo

suspiret: "Eheu, ne rudis agminum
sponsus lacessat regius asperum
  tactu leonem, quem cruenta
    per medias rapit ira caedes."

Dulce et decorum est pro patria mori:
mors et fugacem persequitur virum,
  nec parcit imbellis iuventae
    poplitibus timidove tergo.

Virtus, repulsae nescia sordidae,
intaminatis fulget honoribus,
  nec sumit aut ponit securis
    arbitrio popularis aurae.

Virtus, recludens immeritis mori
caelum, negata temptat iter via,
  coetusque vulgaris et udam
    spernit humum fugiente penna.

Est et fideli tuta silentio
merces. Vetabo qui Cereris sacrum
  vulgarit arcanae sub isdem
    sit trabibus fragilemque mecum

solvat phaselon; saepe Diespiter
neglectus incesto addidit integrum,
  raro antecedentem scelestum
    deseruit pede Poena claudo.

May the young Roman be toughened by experience,
Disciplined in the field, and able to bear
Hardship without complaint, and may he learn
To terrify the terrifying Parthian.

May he spend his days out under the open sky
Doing the work of war. May the young virgin,
With her royal mother on the enemy walls
Watching the furious battle rage, cry out,

Frantic in fear for the life of her fiancé:
"Alas, let not my young unready man,
O let him not arouse that lion's thirst
Making its way toward his body through the fight."

Sweet and proper it is to die for your country,
But Death would just as soon come after him
Who runs away; Death gets him by the backs
Of his fleeing knees and jumps him from behind.

Virtue, rejecting everything that's sordid,
Shines with unblemished honor, nor takes up office
Nor puts it down persuaded by any shift
Of the popular wind; virtue shows the way

To those who deserve to know it, disdaining the crowd,
Taking its flight to heaven on scornful wings;
And he who knows what good faith means, he too
Will be rewarded. I would not sleep beneath

The selfsame roof nor venture to go on board
The selfsame perilous ship as the man who knows
The secret rites and mysteries of Ceres
And can't be trusted with them. Jupiter,

Enraged, might strike the innocent with the guilty.
But in the end it will all be sorted out:
The guilty have a head start, and retribution
Is always slow of foot, but it catches up.

Iustum et tenacem propositi virum
non civium ardor prava iubentium,
    non vultus instantis tyranni
        mente quatit solida neque Auster,

dux inquieti turbidus Hadriae,
nec fulminantis magna manus Iovis;
    si fractus illabatur orbis,
        impavidum ferient ruinae.

Hac arte Pollux et vagus Hercules
enisus arces attigit igneas,
    quos inter Augustus recumbens
        purpureo bibet ore nectar.

Hac te merentem, Bacche pater, tuae
vexere tigres, indocili iugum
    collo trahentes; hac Quirinus
        Martis equis Acheronta fugit,

gratum elocuta consiliantibus
Iunone divis: "Ilion, Ilion
    fatalis incestusque iudex
        et mulier peregrina vertit

in pulverem, ex quo destituit deos
mercede pacta Laomedon, mihi
    castaeque damnatum Minervae
        cum populo et duce fraudulento.

Iam nec Lacaenae splendet adulterae
famosus hospes nec Priami domus
    periura pugnaces Achivos
        Hectoreïs opibus refringit,

nostrisque ductum seditionibus
bellum resedit. Protinus et gravis
    iras et invisum nepotem,
        Troica quem peperit sacerdos,

The man who knows what's right and is tenacious
In the knowledge of what he knows cannot be shaken,
Not by people righteously impassioned
In a wrong cause, and not by menacings

Of tyrants' frowns, nor by the wind that roils
The stormy Adriatic, nor by the fiery
Hand of thundering Jove: the sky could fall
In pieces all around him, he would not quail.

This is how Pollux and Hercules made their way
Up to the stars, where someday Caesar will sit,
Drinking the nectar of heaven, at the same table.
And, Father Bacchus, this is the reason the tigers,

Unused to wearing the yoke, consented to wear it
To draw you in your chariot up the skies;
This is how Romulus, in the chariot
Of Mars, who was his father, was carried up

From Acheron to heaven to be a god.
When the gods in council met to consider the question
Of Romulus' admission among their number,
The goddess Juno spoke, saying these words:

"Troy, O fallen Troy, the foreign woman
And the corrupted judge have brought you down,
Into my hands and the hands of chaste Minerva,
O Troy destined long since to be brought down,

When Priam's royal father broke his promise.
No longer are the eyes of the adulterous
Spartan woman dazzled by the beauty
Of the infamous guest in her husband's house; no longer

Does Hector's help help Priam's house hold out
Against the bellicose Greeks. The war the quarrels
Between the gods kept going is finally over.
From now on I, Juno the goddess, forgive

Marti redonabo; illum ego lucidas
inire sedes, discere nectaris
    sucos et adscribi quietis
        ordinibus patiar deorum.

Dum longus inter saeviat Ilion
Romamque pontus, qualibet exsules
    in parte regnanto beati;
        dum Priami Paridisque busto

insultet armentum et catulos ferae
celent inultae, stet Capitolium
    fulgens triumphatisque possit
        Roma ferox dare iura Medis.

Horrenda late nomen in ultimas
extendat oras, qua medius liquor
    secernit Europen ab Afro,
        qua tumidus rigat arva Nilus.

Aurum irrepertum et sic melius situm,
cum terra celat, spernere fortior
    quam cogere humanos in usus
        omne sacrum rapiente dextra,

quicumque mundo terminus obstitit,
hunc tanget armis, visere gestiens
    qua parte debacchentur ignes,
        qua nebulae pluviique rores.

Sed bellicosis fata Quiritibus
hac lege dico, ne nimium pii
    rebusque fidentes avitae
        tecta velint reparare Troiae.

Troiae renascens alite lugubri
fortuna tristi clade iterabitur,
    ducente victrices catervas
        coniuge me Iovis et sorore.

The offenses that were the cause of Juno's wrath,
And now I consent that the child of Mars, my grandchild,
The child whom the Trojan priestess Ilia bore,
Be permitted to enter into heaven's precincts,

To sit at the table of the serene gods,
To drink the nectar, and be one of them.
I will forgive so long as the deep sea seethes
Forever separating Troy and Rome.

Let the exiles settle and prosper where they will,
So long as cattle are free to trample on
The graves of Priam and of Paris too,
And wild beasts able to whelp and litter there.

This being so, so long may the Capitol shine,
So long may the warlike Romans in their triumph
Lay down the Roman law to the conquered Medes.
Let the name of Rome be heard across the sea,

Over to Egypt where the great river swells
To feed the thirsty fields; let her name resound
To the farthest places, engendering awe and fear.
Let the Romans go to the limits of the world,

Not for the sake of plunder but for the sake
Of extending Roman knowledge everywhere,
From the dervish heat of the desert raving and dancing
To the dripping mists and fogs of the northern swamps.

On this condition only do I promise:
Let not the Romans, over-confident,
And out of misplaced filial piety,
Restore the towers and walls of fallen Troy.

The restoration of Troy could only be
Under the mournful sign of another doom
Brought down upon it by a vengeful host.
Juno herself, Jove's sister-wife, will lead it.

Ter si resurgat murus aëneus
auctore Phoebo, ter pereat meis
    excisus Argivis, ter uxor
        capta virum puerosque ploret."

Non hoc iocosae conveniet lyrae:
quo, Musa, tendis? Desine pervicax
    referre sermones deorum et
        magna modis tenuare parvis.

If yet again, with Apollo's help, the walls
Of Troy should rise in bronze, then yet again,
With Juno's help, the walls of Troy will fall;
And yet again the wives and mothers will weep."

—Why does the Muse persist in telling stories
Of the councils of the gods and such high things
Accompanied by the attenuating sounds
Of my jocund lyre unsuitable for this?

iii.4

Descende caelo et dic age tibia
regina longum Calliope melos,
    seu voce nunc mavis acuta
        seu fidibus citharave Phoebi.

Auditis, an me ludit amabilis
insania? Audire et videor pios
    errare per lucos, amoenae
        quos et aquae subeunt et aurae.

Me fabulosae Vulture in Apulo
nutricis extra limina Pulliae
    ludo fatigatumque somno
        fronde nova puerum palumbes

texere, mirum quod foret omnibus,
quicumque celsae nidum Acherontiae
    saltusque Bantinos et arvum
        pingue tenent humilis Forenti,

ut tuto ab atris corpore viperis
dormirem et ursis, ut premerer sacra
    lauroque collataque myrto,
        non sine dis animosus infans.

Vester, Camenae, vester in arduos
tollor Sabinos, seu mihi frigidum
    Praeneste seu Tibur supinum
        seu liquidae placuere Baiae.

Vestris amicum fontibus et choris
non me Philippis versa acies retro,
    devota non extinxit arbor,
        nec Sicula Palinurus unda.

Utcumque mecum vos eritis, libens
insanientem navita Bosphorum
    temptabo et urentis harenas
        litoris Assyrii viator;

Come down from heaven, Calliope, and play
Upon the flute a lingering melody,
Or unaccompanied sing, in clearest voice,
Or accompanied by the strings of Apollo's lyre.

Companions, do you hear her too, or does
Some pleasing day dream play with me? Do I,
As I think I do, wander upon a sacred
Landscape where the quiet sound of hidden

Waters can be heard, and breezes stir?
When I was a child I strayed out to the slopes
Of Mount Voltore, out beyond the limits
Prescribed for me by Pullia my nurse,

And when I tired of playing and fell asleep,
Why then the guardian doves spread over me
A blanket of fallen leaves, and all the dwellers
In the villages around—high Acherontia,

Bantia in the woods, and low Forentum—
Were full of wonder, I slept so unafraid,
Covered with bay and myrtle, safe and sound
From any harm from any bears or vipers.

These days I take myself, your child, O Muses,
Up to the lofty heights of my Sabine hills,
Or over to cool Praeneste, or Tibur's side,
Or sunny Baiae, wherever I choose to go.

Companion of your waterfalls and choirs,
I could go anywhere: I came away
Unscathed from Philippi, and the falling tree,
And the giant wave near Palinurus Head.

So long as you are with me I will gladly
Set foot on board as a fearless sailor on
The furious Bosporus, or gladly wander
Over the burning sands of Syria,

visam Britannos hospitibus feros
et laetum equino sanguine Concanum,
 visam pharetratos Gelonos
  et Scythicum inviolatus amnem.

Vos Caesarem altum, militia simul
fessas cohortes abdidit oppidis,
 finire quaerentem labores,
  Pierio recreatis antro.

Vos lene consilium et datis et dato
gaudetis, almae. Scimus, ut impios
 Titanas immanemque turbam
  fulmine sustulerit caduco,

qui terram inertem, qui mare temperat
ventosum et urbes regnaque tristia,
 divosque mortalisque turmas
  imperio regit unus aequo.

Magnum illa terrorem intulerat Iovi
fidens iuventus horrida bracchiis
 fratresque tendentes opaco
  Pelion imposuisse Olympo.

Sed quid Typhoeus et validus Mimas,
aut quid minaci Porphyrion statu,
 quid Rhoetus evolsisque truncis
  Enceladus iaculator audax

contra sonantem Palladis aegida
possent ruentes? Hinc avidus stetit
 Vulcanus, hinc matrona Iuno et
  numquam umeris positurus arcum,

qui rore puro Castaliae lavit
crinis solutos, qui Lyciae tenet
 dumeta natalemque silvam,
  Delius et Patareus Apollo.

Safely visit the inhospitable Britons,
The Geloni with their arrows, the Scythians
Who drink the Don, or the Concanians
Who are said to love to drink the blood of horses.

It is you, O Muses, who refreshed our Caesar
With the waters of some cool Pierian grotto,
When having sent away his weary troops
To settle in their towns, he took his ease.

You goddesses who give the gentlest counsel
And take delight in having given it,
You know the story of how the Titans and
Their monstrous cohort were struck down by the lightning-

Bolt of the god who rules the massy earth,
The windy sea, all cities, and the realms
Of shadow underground; for he alone
Is final governor of gods and men.

That upstart gang waving their many hands
Brought horrifying war on Jupiter
As did the brothers determined to pile up mountains,
Mountain on top of mountain, making chaos,

Pelion on Ossa on Olympus.
But what could Typhoeus do, or monstrous Mimas,
Porphyrion grimacing, Rhoetus, or
Enceladus hurling trees torn up by the roots,

What could they do against the chiming shield
Of Pallas Athena? Vulcan was there beside her,
Avid for victory, Juno was there, and Apollo
Whose bow is ever ready at his shoulder,

The god who bathes his unbound flowing hair
In the stream that flows out from the Castalian spring,
The god who haunts the wood of Lycia and
The hill on the isle of Delos where he was born.

Vis consili expers mole ruit sua:
vim temperatam di quoque provehunt
    in maius; idem odere viris
        omne nefas animo moventis.

Testis mearum centimanus Gyas
sententiarum, notus et integrae
    temptator Orion Dianae,
        virginea domitus sagitta.

Iniecta monstris Terra dolet suis
maeretque partus fulmine luridum
    missos ad Orcum; nec peredit
        impositam celer ignis Aetnen,

incontinentis nec Tityi iecur
reliquit ales, nequitiae additus
    custos; amatorem trecentae
        Pirithoum cohibent catenae.

Strength without wisdom falls by its own weight;
The strength that wisdom tempers, the gods increase;
The gods abhor that strength whose heart knows nothing
But what impiety is, and it is punished.

Hundred-handed Gyas has reason to know
The meaning of what I say, and so has Orion,
Who sought to tempt the chaste goddess Diana.
She therefore struck him down with her chastening arrow.

Earth lying upon their fallen bodies groans
And mutters in her grief for her monstrous brood,
Sent down to ghastly Orcus by Jupiter's lightning.
Nor has the fire finished eating its way

Through Aetna's innards yet; nor has the vulture
Who watches over Tityos' tortured lust
Finished its meal of his liver; and he who sought
To take Proserpina still lies in chains.

Caelo tonantem credidimus Iovem
regnare; praesens divus habebitur
  Augustus adiectis Britannis
    imperio gravibusque Persis.

Milesne Crassi coniuge barbara
turpis maritus vixit et hostium
  (pro curia inversique mores!)
    consenuit socerorum in armis

sub rege Medo, Marsus et Apulus,
anciliorum et nominis et togae
  oblitus aeternaeque Vestae,
    incolumi Iove et urbe Roma?

Hoc caverat mens provida Reguli
dissentientis condicionibus
  foedis et exemplo trahentis
    perniciem veniens in aevum,

si non periret immiserabilis
captiva pubes. "Signa ego Punicis
  affixa delubris et arma
    militibus sine caede" dixit

"derepta vidi; vidi ego civium
retorta tergo bracchia libero
  portasque non clausas et arva
    Marte coli populata nostro.

The way we know that Jove is king in heaven
Is by his manifestation in what he does.
Listen! Jove is thundering in the sky.
Augustus too will show his godlike power

In what he does: and so the Britons will be
Put down by him, and the frightening Medes also.
Is it not true that soldiers of Crassus's army
Lowered themselves to marry barbarian wives

(O Rome disgraced in such disgraceful ways!)
And served their time out in the army of
Their fathers-in-law, the enemies of Rome?
Imagine! Roman soldiers willing to serve

Under the orders of Medes, forgetting that
They bore the name of Roman, forgetting about
The temple of Vesta and the sacred shields,
Although their city still needed their defense.

This is what Regulus saw and why he refused
To accept the bargain of easy shameful terms.
He saw that a peace thus bargained for would be
A precedent for how the glory of Rome

Would come in future days to final ruin,
Unless our Roman soldiers, if they are captured,
Are left—to die if they must—in the enemy camp.
"With my own eyes," he said, "I have seen our banners

Hung up in shame on the walls in Punic shrines,
And I have seen our weapons given over
Without a struggle into Punic hands;
With my own eyes I have seen our young men standing,

Their arms pinioned in shame behind their backs,
The gates of Carthage confidently open,
Unthreatened now, the fields once scorched by us
Now growing their peaceful grain, fearless of Rome.

Auro repensus scilicet acrior
miles redibit. Flagitio additis
    damnum: neque amissos colores
        lana refert medicata fuco,

nec vera virtus, cum semel excidit,
curat reponi deterioribus.
    Si pugnat extricata densis
        cerva plagis, erit ille fortis

qui perfidis se credidit hostibus,
et Marte Poenos proteret altero,
    qui lora restrictis lacertis
        sensit iners timuitque mortem.

Hic, unde vitam sumeret inscius,
pacem duello miscuit. O pudor!
    O magna Carthago, probrosis
        altior Italiae ruinis!"

Fertur pudicae coniugis osculum
parvosque natos ut capitis minor
    ab se removisse et virilem
        torvus humi posuisse vultum,

donec labantis consilio patres
firmaret auctor numquam alias dato,
    interque maerentis amicos
        egregius properaret exsul.

Atqui sciebat quae sibi barbarus
tortor pararet. Non aliter tamen
    dimovit obstantis propinquos
        et populum reditus morantem,

quam si clientum longa negotia
diiudicata lite relinqueret,
    tendens Venafranos in agros
        aut Lacedaemonium Tarentum.

What makes you think that he, the ransomed soldier,
Brought safely back to Rome by payment of gold
Will bravely fight in battle a second time?
What makes you think he will get his manhood back

Once he has stood tied up there, trembling with fear?
A man like that, confused about who he is,
Confuses peace and war. O shame of Rome!
O greatness of Carthage built on Roman shame!"

It is said that Regulus shunned his wife's embraces
And the kisses of his weeping little children,
As if he had no right to them, and stood,
Eyes gazing fixed upon the ground, as waiting

For the wavering Roman Fathers in their Senate
To come to understand his argument.
And then—oh yes, he knew that torture and death
Were ready for him when he went back to Carthage,

As he had promised—Regulus shouldered his way
Through the protesting crowd of friends and relations,
Looking as if he had just completed a case
In court or some other tedious legal chore,

And was off for a weekend at his place in the country.

iii.6

Delicta maiorum immeritus lues,
Romane, donec templa refeceris
  aedisque labentis deorum et
    foeda nigro simulacra fumo.

Dis te minorem quod geris, imperas:
hinc omne principium; huc refer exitum.
  Di multa neglecti dederunt
    Hesperiae mala luctuosae.

Iam bis Monaeses et Pacori manus
inauspicatos contudit impetus
  nostros et adiecisse praedam
    torquibus exiguis renidet.

Paene occupatam seditionibus
delevit urbem Dacus et Aethiops,
  hic classe formidatus, ille
    missilibus melior sagittis.

Fecunda culpae saecula nuptias
primum inquinavere et genus et domos;
  hoc fonte derivata clades
    in patriam populumque fluxit.

It's not a question of whether or not you're guilty,
  Roman, yourself.
The transgressions of your fathers must be paid for.
  You must rebuild
The broken-down temples and the toppled altars;
  You must restore,
Also, the fallen statues, cleaned of their grime.

The only way to rule is to serve the gods.
  All things begin
From them; and it is only the gods who know
  How all things end.
Neglected, the gods brought down upon the Romans
  All the misfortunes
Sorrowing Italy suffers from in these days.

Twice now the Parthians have crushed our army,
  Turning us back
Under a bad star's sign; how they must grin,
  The Parthian warriors,
So pleased to have added Roman trophies to all
  The others that dangle
And glitter on their savage necklaces.

Confused, bewildered by internal conflict,
  The city of Rome
Just barely escaped destruction by the Dacians,
  Formidable and fearsome
Because of the skills of their famous ranks of archers,
  Or by the Egyptians,
Formidable as they, but because of their ships.

Prolific with vileness this generation has soiled
  The marriage bed,
And then corrupted the children in the home;
  And from this source,
Reeking, polluted, and degenerate,
  Calamity
Flows out infecting everything there is

Motus doceri gaudet Ionicos
matura virgo et fingitur artibus
    iam nunc et incestos amores
        de tenero meditatur ungui.

Mox iuniores quaerit adulteros
inter mariti vina, neque eligit
    cui donet impermissa raptim
        gaudia luminibus remotis,

sed iussa coram non sine conscio
surgit marito, seu vocat institor
    seu navis Hispanae magister,
        dedecorum pretiosus emptor.

Non his iuventus orta parentibus
infecit aequor sanguine Punico
    Pyrrhumque et ingentem cecidit
        Antiochum Hannibalemque dirum;

sed rusticorum mascula militum
proles, Sabellis docta ligonibus
    versare glaebas et severae
        matris ad arbitrium recisos

portare fustis, sol ubi montium
mutaret umbras et iuga demeret
    bobus fatigatis, amicum
        tempus agens abeunte curru.

Damnosa quid non imminuit dies?
Aetas parentum, peior avis, tulit
    nos nequiores, mox daturos
        progeniem vitiosiorem.

In the Roman state. The young woman eager for love
    And eager for pleasure
First takes her pleasure in learning how to dance
    In the lascivious
Grecian way, and practices her skills,
    Her mind alive
With images of the unchaste loves to come.

It isn't long before, in her husband's house,
    At the drinking parties,
She's on the lookout, and not without his knowledge,
    For younger lovers,
Nor is she choosy about whoever it is
    When the lights are low,
Some visiting salesman, maybe, or maybe some Spanish

Ship captain or other. Dealers in shame. In the old days,
    The days of the fathers
Of those because of whom the sea ran red
    With Punic blood,
And those because of whom Antiochus fell,
    And Hannibal
The Terrible, it wasn't like this. Those virtuous

Romans were taught how to use the Sabine hoe
    To till the soil
Of their father's farm and at their mother's call
    To carry in
The cut wood when on the hill the shadows shifted
    As the sun went down.
It was the hour of rest for man and beast.

What is there that has been left unruined?
    Our parents' time
Was worse than was their parents' time, and then
    They brought forth us,
Worse than they were, and after us will be
    Our sons and daughters,
Worse than we are, then theirs, still worse than they.

iii.7

Quid fles, Asterie, quem tibi candidi
primo restituent vere Favonii
    Thyna merce beatum,
        constantis iuvenem fide,

Gygen? Ille Notis actus ad Oricum
post insana Caprae sidera frigidas
    noctes non sine multis
        insomnis lacrimis agit.

Atqui sollicitae nuntius hospitae,
suspirare Chloen et miseram tuis
    dicens ignibus uri,
        temptat mille vafer modis.

Ut Proetum mulier perfida credulum
falsis impulerit criminibus nimis
    casto Bellerophontae
        maturare necem refert;

narrat paene datum Pelea Tartaro,
Magnessam Hippolyten dum fugit abstinens;
    et peccare docentis
        fallax historias monet.

Frustra: nam scopulis surdior Icari
voces audit adhuc integer. At tibi
    ne vicinus Enipeus
        plus iusto placeat cave;

quamvis non alius flectere equum sciens
aeque conspicitur gramine Martio,
    nec quisquam citus aeque
        Tusco denatat alveo.

Asteria, why are you weeping?
  The clearing skies and brightening winds of Spring
Will bring your faithful Gyges home to you,
  With many gifts from Bithynia.

Gyges, driven ashore
  At Oricum by the storm that the Wild Goat
Constellation was the cause of, weeps,
  Alone, through the sleepless night.

Meanwhile though, somebody sent
  By his lovesick hostess, Chloë, telling about
How Chloë weeps and sighs and burns for him,
  Tempts him with many stories.

This messenger tells him about
  How a lying woman with lying stories got
Proetus to plot to kill Bellerophon,
  Bellerophon the chaste;

Also she tells him about
  Peleus, and how Hippolyta, who loved him,
Told lies about him and almost got *him* killed;
  And she tells him other stories,

All of them part of the plan
  To teach poor Gyges how not to be chaste Gyges.
In vain. So far at least, he is deaf as a cliff
  To the sound of her echoing voice

Telling him lying stories.
  Duplicitous. But, Asteria, be careful
That your neighbor Enipeus doesn't please you
  More than he ought to please you.

There isn't a better rider
  Or a better-looking rider on the Campus;
Or a better swimmer swimming in the Tiber.
  Close up your house at night.

Prima nocte domum claude neque in vias
sub cantu querulae despice tibiae,
　　et te saepe vocanti
　　　　duram difficilis mane.

You must be very careful
    Not to come near your window when you hear
His plaintive song about how cruel you are
    And how he longs for you only.

iii.8

Martiis caelebs quid agam Kalendis,
quid velint flores et acerra turis
plena miraris positusque carbo in
    caespite vivo,

docte sermones utriusque linguae?
Voveram dulcis epulas et album
Libero caprum prope funeratus
    arboris ictu.

Hic dies anno redeunte festus
corticem adstrictum pice dimovebit
amphorae fumum bibere institutae
    consule Tullo.

Sume, Maecenas, cyathos amici
sospitis centum et vigiles lucernas
perfer in lucem; procul omnis esto
    clamor et ira.

Mitte civilis super urbe curas:
occidit Daci Cotisonis agmen,
Medus infestus sibi luctuosis
    dissidet armis,

servit Hispanae vetus hostis orae
Cantaber, sera domitus catena,
iam Scythae laxo meditantur arcu
    cedere campis.

Neglegens ne qua populus laboret,
parce privatus nimium cavere et
dona praesentis cape laetus horae ac
    linque severa.

iii.8 / *To Maecenas*

What in the world is an old bachelor doing,
On the Kalends of March, supposed to be reserved
For celebrating marriage and things like that?
   Why, you ask, the flowers,

And why the incense, and why the turf and embers
Ready for the incense to be lit?
I promised Bacchus I would sacrifice
   A pure white goat to him

And that I'd give a party every year
Because he saved me from death by falling tree.
I promised to open a jar of the finest wine,
   Dating from Tullus's time.

Therefore, Maecenas, come, let's celebrate
How I escaped with my life. Let's drink a lot.
Let's keep the torches lighted until dawn,
   And banish all contention.

Give up for a while your worries about the world.
Cotiso's Dacian army has bit the dust;
Our enemies the bloody Parthians
   Are bloodying one another;

The Cantabrians in Spain at last are wearing
The chains of servitude to Rome; the Scythians
Are thinking of decamping from their plains,
   Their deadly bows unstrung.

Accept the gift of pleasure when it's given.
Be willing for now to be a private person,
Unworried about the city and how it's doing.
   Put serious things aside.

iii.9

"Donec gratus eram tibi
  nec quisquam potior bracchia candidae
cervici iuvenis dabat,
  Persarum vigui rege beatior."

"Donec non alia magis
  arsisti neque erat Lydia post Chloën,
multi Lydia nominis
  Romana vigui clarior Ilia."

"Me nunc Thressa Chloë regit,
  dulcis docta modos et citharae sciens,
pro qua non metuam mori
  si parcent animae fata superstiti."

"Me torret face mutua
  Thurini Calaïs filius Ornyti,
pro quo bis patiar mori,
  si parcent puero fata superstiti."

"Quid si prisca redit Venus
  diductosque iugo cogit aëneo?
si flava excutitur Chloë
  reiectaeque patet ianua Lydiae?"

"Quamquam sidere pulchrior
  ille est, tu levior cortice et improbo
iracundior Hadria,
  tecum vivere amem, tecum obeam libens!"

"When you loved me the best
  And I thought there was nobody else,
Before you preferred to mine
  Calais' arms around
Your beautiful shoulders, then,
  I was happy as can be,
Happier than the King
  Of Persia is, I was."

"When you loved me the best
  And I thought there was nobody else,
And Chloë wasn't first
  On the list in your heart (I was),
Why then I thought I was
  The toast of everyone;
I was happier than Mars'
  Beloved Ilia was."

"Now I love Chloë best,
  Chloë, whose singing and
Her playing on the lyre
  Charms everyone who hears her.
Chloë is the one
  I'd die for if I had to,
If the Fates would only spare her
  To live happily ever after."

"I love Calais best,
  Who is Ornytus' son;
Calais loves me too;
  It's entirely mutual.
Calais is the one
  I would die for if I had to,
If the Fates would only allow him
  To live happily ever after."

"What if Venus took it
  Into her head to join
Together once again

Those whom she had parted?
How would it be if lovely
   Chloë were shown the door,
And the door were left wide-open
   For Lydia to come back in?"

"Calais is fairer than
   Any star in the sky;
And you are lighter than
   A cork bobbing upon
The waters of the stormy
   Adriatic Sea—
But if you say you love me
   I'll love you truly forever."

Extremum Tanaïn si biberes, Lyce,
saevo nupta viro, me tamen asperas
porrectum ante fores obicere incolis
    plorares Aquilonibus.

Audis, quo strepitu ianua, quo nemus
inter pulchra satum tecta remugiat
ventis, et positas ut glaciet nives
    puro numine Iuppiter?

Ingratam Veneri pone superbiam,
ne currente retro funis eat rota;
non te Penelopen difficilem procis
    Tyrrhenus genuit parens.

O quamvis neque te munera nec preces
nec tinctus viola pallor amantium
nec vir Pieria paelice saucius
    curvat, supplicibus tuis

parcas, nec rigida mollior aesculo
nec Mauris animum mitior anguibus.
Non hoc semper erit liminis aut aquae
    caelestis patiens latus.

Lycia, just suppose the icy water
Of the River Don were the water that you drank
Every day of the week. Suppose that you
Were married to some Scythian tyrant husband.

Even if that were true you wouldn't have
The heart to leave me out in the cold like this,
Lying across your doorstep in the wind.
Don't you hear how loudly the suffering trees are groaning

Out in your frozen garden? And don't you hear
The rattling of your doors? And don't you see
How Jupiter's icy light in the cloudless night
Glitters across the surface of the snow?

Give up your cruel disdain, which Venus hates,
Lest the rope run backward as the wheel does too.
Everyone knows you're no Penelope.
Your parents didn't raise you to be like her.

Though neither prayers, nor presents, nor your suitors'
Pale stricken faces move you, nor your husband's
Carrying on with his mistress, still, have mercy.
I know it's about as easy for you to bend

As for an oak to bend, you with a heart
As cold as the heart of a snake. How long do you think
That I'll be able to bear it, out here on your threshold,
Tormented like this, out in the winter weather?

iii.11

Mercuri (nam te docilis magistro
movit Amphion lapides canendo),
tuque testudo resonare septem
    callida nervis,

nec loquax olim neque grata, nunc et
divitum mensis et amica templis,
dic modos, Lyde quibus obstinatas
    applicet auris,

quae velut latis equa trima campis
ludit exsultim metuitque tangi,
nuptiarum expers et adhuc protervo
    cruda marito.

Tu potes tigris comitesque silvas
ducere et rivos celeres morari;
cessit immanis tibi blandienti
    ianitor aulae

Cerberus, quamvis furiale centum
muniant angues caput eius atque
spiritus taeter saniesque manet
    ore trilingui.

Quin et Ixion Tityosque vultu
risit invito, stetit urna paulum
sicca, dum grato Danaï puellas
    carmine mulces.

O Mercury who taught
  Amphion how to make
The very stones arise
  And move and take their place,
And thou O turtle shell
  Which at one time could neither
Speak nor please the ear,
  Now with your seven strings
Welcome at rich men's feasts
  And also in the temples,
Invent such music as
  Will make young Lyde listen.
She's like a little filly
  Out in the far fields playing,
Three years old and wary,
  Unready yet to marry,
Shying away from man.
  You have the power to lead
A company of tigers
  Tamely through a wood.
You have the power to make
  A flowing stream stand still
In order to hear your music.
  Your music softened the heart
Of Cerberus the ferocious
  Keeper of the door
Of the entrance into hell,
  Although around his head
A hundred serpents writhed,
  And vile smelly matter
Slavered from his three-
  Tongued bloody mouth.
Tityos and Ixion
  When they heard your music
Could not help but smile
  Though under grievous torture,
And for a time the urn
  Was dry while Danaus' daughters
Listened to your song.

Audiat Lyde scelus atque notas
virginum poenas et inane lymphae
dolium fundo pereuntis imo
    seraque fata,

quae manent culpas etiam sub Orco.
Impiae (nam quid potuere maius?)
impiae sponsos potuere duro
    perdere ferro.

Una de multis face nuptuali
digna periurum fuit in parentem
splendide mendax et in omne virgo
    nobilis aevum,

"Surge" quae dixit iuveni marito,
"surge, ne longus tibi somnus, unde
non times, detur; socerum et scelestas
    falle sorores,

Let Lyde be told the story
Of what these daughters did
    And how they are punished forever;
Let her be told the story
    Of the bottomless empty urn
They evermore must pour
    The vanishing water into,
Which vanishes forever
    From the urn forever empty.
Let her be told what happens
    To guilty ones sooner or later
In Orcus's dark kingdom.

    These impious wives—
What worse could they have done
    Than what they did that night?—
These impious wives,
    Faithful to their father,
Took up their cruel knives
    And killed their youthful husbands
Sleeping in the night.
    But there was one of the sisters
Worthily true to the vows
    Of the sanctity of marriage
And, unlike her sisters,
    Worthily false to her father.
She said in the night to her youthful
    Husband as he slept,
"Awake, for sleeping you
    Do not know what my father
And his daughters my wicked sisters
    Have planned for you in the night.
Awake, and leave this place,
    Escape, for, as I speak,
Like lionesses they,
    Falling upon young steers,
These sisters with their knives
    Fall upon their husbands
And slaughter them as they sleep.

quae, velut nanctae vitulos leaenae,
singulos eheu lacerant. Ego illis
mollior nec te feriam neque intra
    claustra tenebo.

Me pater saevis oneret catenis,
quod viro clemens misero peperci;
me vel extremos Numidarum in agros
    classe releget.

I, pedes quo te rapiunt et aurae,
dum favet Nox et Venus; i secundo
omine et nostri memorem sepulcro
    scalpe querelam."

I, who am other than they,
Will do no harm to you,
  Nor will I keep you here.
Awake, and leave this place,
  Escape while still you may.
Let my father bind my body
  In the cruel chains of torture,
Or let my father send me
  To die in the farthest reaches
Of the Numidian desert.
  While Night and Venus favor,
Leave this place and go
  Wherever fortune takes you
By foot or else by sea.
  May the gods be kind to you.
And someday write my story
  Upon my sepulcher."

iii.12

Miserarum est neque amori dare ludum neque dulci
mala vino lavere aut exanimari metuentis
  patruae verbera linguae.

Tibi qualum Cythereae puer ales, tibi telas
operosaeque Minervae studium aufert, Neobule,
  Liparaeï nitor Hebri,

simul unctos Tiberinis umeros lavit in undis,
eques ipso melior Bellerophonte, neque pugno
  neque segni pede victus,

catus idem per apertum fugientis agitato
grege cervos iaculari et celer arto latitantem
  fruticeto excipere aprum.

That girl is in a very
　Sad situation

Who hasn't become a player,
　Yet, in the game of love;

Who isn't even allowed—
　Still under the thumb

Of some censorious uncle—
　To have even a taste

Of the very weakest wine.
　Cupid, the wingèd child

Of Venus, goddess of love,
　Runs off with your wool-basket

And with your weaving, too,
　And with them with your devotion

To household duty and
　The diligent goddess Minerva,

When you catch sight of the shining
　Shoulders of Hebrus as

He comes up out of the Tiber
　After a morning swim.

He's a better rider than
　Bellerophon ever was;

He's an undefeated boxer;
　A winning runner too;

He's the best spearsman there is
　When across the field a stag

Flees with the wild-eyed herd;
   And just as good at spearing

The savage boar that hides
   In the dark thicket waiting.

iii.13

O fons Bandusiae, splendidior vitro,
dulci digne mero non sine floribus,
    cras donaberis haedo,
        cui frons turgida cornibus

primis et venerem et proelia destinat.
Frustra: nam gelidos inficiet tibi
    rubro sanguine rivos
        lascivi suboles gregis.

Te flagrantis atrox hora Caniculae
nescit tangere, tu frigus amabile
    fessis vomere tauris
        praebes et pecori vago.

Fies nobilium tu quoque fontium,
me dicente cavis impositam ilicem
    saxis, unde loquaces
        lymphae desiliunt tuae.

O clearer than crystal, thou Bandusian fountain,
To whom it is fitting to bring libations of wine

And offerings also of flowers, tomorrow the chosen
First-born of the flock will be brought to you,

His new little horns foretelling warfare and love
In vain, for the warm blood of this child of the flock

Will stain with its color of red your clear cold waters.
The cruel heat of Canicula the Dog Star

Can find no way to penetrate the glade
To where you are. Gladly your shady coolness

Welcomes the oxen that come, weary of plowing,
And welcomes also the wandering pasturing flock.

You shall become famous among the fountains
Because of my song that praises the ilex tree

That leans above the rocks the babbling waters leap from.

iii.14

Herculis ritu modo dictus, o plebs,
morte venalem petiisse laurum
Caesar Hispana repetit penatis
    victor ab ora.

Unico gaudens mulier marito
prodeat iustis operata divis
et soror clari ducis et decorae
    supplice vitta

virginum matres iuvenumque nuper
sospitum. Vos, o pueri et puellae
iam virum expertae, male ominatis
    parcite verbis.

Hic dies vere mihi festus atras
eximet curas; ego nec tumultum
nec mori per vim metuam tenente
    Caesare terras.

I pete unguentum, puer, et coronas
et cadum Marsi memorem duelli,
Spartacum si qua potuit vagantem
    fallere testa.

Dic et argutae properet Neaerae
murreum nodo cohibere crinem;
si per invisum mora ianitorem
    fiet, abito.

Lenit albescens animos capillus
litium et rixae cupidos protervae;
non ego hoc ferrem calidus iuventa
    consule Planco.

It's said of Caesar that, like Hercules,
He sought his fame at the risk of seeking death.
And so he did. And now, triumphant, he
Comes home from Spain to his household's joyful welcome.

Having made grateful sacrifice to the gods,
His wife comes forward to greet her unequaled husband,
And then the sister, and, decked with grateful garlands,
The mothers of virgins and of the young men whom

The victory in the war has spared. May you,
You youngest boys and girls, now celebrate
The day of his return with decorous hymns.
Let there be no ill omens in your song.

This day will be a festive day for me;
No longer will I fear a civil war
Nor other cause of violent bloody death.
Caesar is in command of all the earth.

Go, boy, bring garlands, and perfumes, too, and bring
A bottle of the vintage wine that dates
From the time of the Marsic War, if there be any
That has survived the marauding Spartacus.

Go ask Neaera, she who sings so well,
To bind her chestnut hair up in a knot,
And hurry to be with us. If the old doorkeeper
Won't let you speak to her, then give it up.

In the days of my youth, in Plancus' consulship,
I never would have put up with such a thing,
But now my time of strife and faction is over.
My white hair calms my warfare-loving spirit.

Uxor pauperis Ibyci,
   tandem nequitiae fige modum tuae
famosisque laboribus;
   maturo propior desine funeri

inter ludere virgines
   et stellis nebulam spargere candidis.
Non, si quid Pholoën, satis
   et te, Chlori, decet: filia rectius

expugnat iuvenem domos,
   pulso Thyias uti concita tympano.
Illam cogit amor Nothi
   lascivae similem ludere capreae;

te lanae prope nobilem
   tonsae Luceriam, non citharae decent
nec flos purpureus rosae
   nec poti vetulam faece tenus cadi.

iii.15 / *To Ibycus's Wife*

Poor old wife of poor old Ibycus,
It's time for you to put a stop to your

Disreputable laborious carryings-on.
It's getting to be quite near the time to die.

You ought to give up acting as if you were
Youthful among the youthful, clouding over

The bright clear stars in the sky the way you do.
What might be right for Pholoë isn't for you;

The mother of the daughter isn't the daughter.
Maybe it's perfectly all right for her

To lay siege to the young men's houses as if she were
A Bacchante whom the pulse of the drum had excited.

True lust for Nothus drives your daughter to play
Like a doe in heat; for you, old girl, the famous

Knitting wool from Luceria is what's right;
What isn't right is the music of the lyre

In an atmosphere of dark red blooming roses,
And the wine-jar emptied in the evening revel.

iii.16

Inclusam Danaën turris aëneä
robustaeque fores et vigilum canum
tristes excubiae munierant satis
    nocturnis ab adulteris,

si non Acrisium virginis abditae
custodem pavidum Iuppiter et Venus
risissent: fore enim tutum iter et patens
    converso in pretium deo.

Aurum per medios ire satellites
et perrumpere amat saxa, potentius
ictu fulmineo; concidit auguris
    Argivi domus, ob lucrum

demersa exitio; diffidit urbium
portas vir Macedo et subruit aemulos
reges muneribus; munera navium
    saevos illaqueant duces.

Crescentem sequitur cura pecuniam
maiorumque fames. Iure perhorrui
late conspicuum tollere verticem,
    Maecenas, equitum decus.

Quanto quisque sibi plura negaverit,
ab dis plura feret: nil cupientium
nudus castra peto et transfuga divitum
    partis linquere gestio,

contemptae dominus splendidior rei,
quam si quicquid arat impiger Apulus
occultare meis dicerer horreis,
    magnas inter opes inops.

Watchdogs watching, thick tower walls, oak doors,
Such things would have been quite sufficient to keep

The lovers of Danaë from getting in
By night to where she was, locked up from them.

But Jupiter and Venus only laughed,
Because they knew the way to get in was easy:

Jupiter had but to turn himself into gold.
Gold loves to get itself past sentinels

And loves to make its way through solid rock.
Gold has more power than Jupiter's lightning-bolts.

Gold brought the house of the Argive prophet down;
Gold given by Philip of Macedon opened the gates

Of cities and made its way beneath the thrones
Of mighty kings, and thus their thrones fell down.

The more the money grows the more the greed
Grows too; also the anxiety of greed.

Maecenas, glory of simple knighthood, this
Is the reason I myself was always afraid

Of too much ambition and of rising too high.
The more a man can do without, the more

The gods will do for him. So, empty-handed,
Deserting the camp of the rich, I seek the camp

Of those who ask for little, and thus I am
A more impressive master of all the wealth

I happily have contempt for than if I
Were that poor thing belittled by his riches,

Purae rivus aquae silvaque iugerum
paucorum et segetis certa fides meae
fulgentem imperio fertilis Africae
    fallit sorte beatior.

Quamquam nec Calabrae mella ferunt apes,
nec Laestrygonia Bacchus in amphora
languescit mihi, nec pinguia Gallicis
    crescunt vellera pascuis,

importuna tamen pauperies abest,
nec, si plura velim, tu dare deneges.
Contracto melius parva cupidine
    vectigalia porrigam,

quam si Mygdoniis regnum Alyattei
campis continuem. Multa petentibus
desunt multa: bene est, cui deus obtulit
    parca quod satis est manu.

Hiding away in his storehouse everything garnered
From the rich Apulian fields his peasants till.

The splendid lord of the riches of Africa
Mistakenly thinks he's better off than I,

With my little farm whose crops I'm certain of,
And my little quiet stream of pure brook water.

I don't have hives of bees from Calabria
Busily making their honey just for me;

I don't have jars of rare Laestrygonian wine
Slowly maturing itself only for me;

I have no Gallic pasturelands where sheep
Are growing their wool exclusively for me.

I don't have poverty, either, to worry about,
And if I were in need of anything more,

I know Maecenas would not deny it to me.
The less I want the more I seem to have.

That's better than if I owned what Midas owned
Combined with everything that Croesus owned.

Want much, lack much. That man has just enough
To whom the gods have given just enough.

Aeli vetusto nobilis ab Lamo—
quando et priores hinc Lamias ferunt
   denominatos et nepotum
      per memores genus omne fastus,

auctore ab illo ducis originem,
qui Formiarum moenia dicitur
   princeps et innantem Maricae
      litoribus tenuisse Lirim,

late tyrannus—cras foliis nemus
multis et alga litus inutili
   demissa tempestas ab Euro
      sternet, aquae nisi fallit augur

annosa cornix. Dum potes, aridum
compone lignum: cras Genium mero
   curabis et porco bimestri
      cum famulis operum solutis.

Aelius, evidently you come down
From that old despot Lamus, or so they say
Who say that everyone having that name can claim
Descent from him who built the Formian walls

And ruled the delta of the river Liris,
Prince of the marshes sacred to Marica.
Tomorrow, unless the raven's wrong—cross old
Foreteller of bad weather—a storm is coming.

Branches will be down in all the groves,
Leaves scattered everywhere, and there will be
Seaweed detritus washed up on all the beaches.
Get firewood into the house to keep it dry.

Tomorrow, have a party with your slaves.
Give them a holiday, have a good time.
Serve up the unadulterated wine,
And a roasted suckling pig, not two months old.

iii.18

Faune, Nympharum fugientum amator,
per meos finis et aprica rura
lenis incedas abeasque parvis
    aequus alumnis,

si tener pleno cadit haedus anno,
larga nec desunt Veneris sodali
vina craterae, vetus ara multo
    fumat odore.

Ludit herboso pecus omne campo,
cum tibi Nonae redeunt Decembres;
festus in pratis vacat otioso
    cum bove pagus;

inter audacis lupus errat agnos;
spargit agrestis tibi silva frondes;
gaudet invisam pepulisse fossor
    ter pede terram.

O Faunus, when, pursuing a nymph in flight,
You come to the edge of the sunny fields of my farm,

Be gentle as you pass across those fields
And in your passing by propitious be

To the nurslings of my flock, I pray, for, when
The fullness of the year comes round again

We celebrate your day and on that day
A tender kid is offered up to you

And in the mixing bowl there's plenty of wine,
That's love's companion, and the incense smoke

Pours out with many odors from the altar,
And all the flocks and herds can play in the fields,

And all the people too, in holiday dress,
Keep holiday among the idle creatures,

Because it is your day; among the lambs,
Who have no fear of him, there is the wolf,

On holiday too, taking a friendly walk
In honor of you; and in your honor, too,

The trees have scattered their leaves upon the ground;
And he whose daily toil it is to dig,

Dances today, stamping his holiday feet
In triple rhythm on the enemy earth.

iii.19

Quantum distet ab Inacho
   Codrus pro patria non timidus mori
narras et genus Aeaci
   et pugnata sacro bella sub Ilio;

quo Chium pretio cadum
   mercemur, quis aquam temperet ignibus,
quo praebente domum et quota
   Paelignis caream frigoribus, taces.

Da lunae propere novae,
   da noctis mediae, da, puer, auguris
Murenae: tribus aut novem
   miscentur cyathis pocula commodis.

Qui Musas amat imparis,
   ternos ter cyathos attonitus petet
vates; tris prohibet supra
   rixarum metuens tangere Gratia

nudis iuncta sororibus.
   Insanire iuvat: cur Berecyntiae
cessant flamina tibiae?
   Cur pendet tacita fistula cum lyra?

Parcentis ego dexteras
   odi: sparge rosas; audiat invidus
dementem strepitum Lycus
   et vicina seni non habilis Lyco.

Spissa te nitidum coma,
   puro te similem, Telephe, vespero
tempestiva petit Rhode;
   me lentus Glycerae torret amor meae.

iii.19 / *To Telephus*

You're good at telling us all the details about
The line of descent from Inachus down to Codrus,
Who had no fear of dying for his country;
And you're also good at telling all the details

Of how the descendants of Aeacus, Jove's own son,
Fought so bravely under the walls of Troy.
But, Telephus, you're no good at all at telling
How much the wine is going to cost, or who

Is going to make the fire to heat the water,
Who's going to give the party, under whose roof
We'll be invited in out of the cold.
Let's have a party. Come, let's celebrate

Murena's augurship and drink his health,
And drink the health of midnight, and the health
Of the new moon. Whether it's three cyathi
Or three times three's a matter of point of view.

The Muse-struck bard of course wants three times three.
The sister Graces, not wanting any trouble,
Think three are quite enough. Where is the music?
Where's the sound of the flute? Why are the pipes

And the silent lyre still hanging on the wall?
Where are the flowers? Let jealous old Lycus next door
Hear the noise of the party starting up, and let
His girlfriend hear it too. Telephus, she

Is much too young for him. She has her eye
On your good looks. With your shining hair she thinks
You're like the shining evening star. And I?
I have my eye on Glycera's good looks.

iii.20

Non vides quanto moveas periclo,
Pyrrhe, Gaetulae catulos leaenae?
Dura post paulo fugies inaudax
    proelia raptor,

cum per obstantis iuvenum catervas
ibit insignem repetens Nearchum:
grande certamen, tibi praeda cedat,
    maior an illa.

Interim, dum tu celeris sagittas
promis, haec dentes acuit timendos,
arbiter pugnae posuisse nudo
    sub pede palmam

fertur et leni recreare vento
sparsum odoratis umerum capillis,
qualis aut Nireus fuit aut aquosa
    raptus ab Ida.

iii.20 / *To Pyrrhus*

Don't you see how dangerous it is
To get too close to the lioness's cub?

It won't be long before you're going to be
An unnerved hero running away from trouble.

When she sets off through the crowd of young men standing
There in the way between him and her, when she's

On the hunt for beautiful Nearchus, then
There's going to be a battle between you two

To find out which of the two of you, you,
Or she, is going to win the prize—meanwhile,

While you are sharpening your weapons, and while she
Is gnashing her fearsome lioness's teeth,

Both of you getting ready, the referee
(Who happens to be the prize) indifferently

Sits cooling his shoulders in the summer breeze.
He looks like Nireus, there in the sunny piazza,

Or Ganymede, with his uncut shining hair,
Who was carried off from near the fountains of Ida.

O nata mecum consule Manlio,
seu tu querelas sive geris iocos
    seu rixam et insanos amores
        seu facilem, pia testa, somnum,

quocumque lectum nomine Massicum
servas, moveri digna bono die,
    descende Corvino iubente
        promere languidiora vina.

Non ille, quamquam Socraticis madet
sermonibus, te negleget horridus:
    narratur et prisci Catonis
        saepe mero caluisse virtus.

Tu lene tormentum ingenio admoves
plerumque duro; tu sapientium
    curas et arcanum iocoso
        consilium retegis Lyaeo;

tu spem reducis mentibus anxiis
viresque et addis cornua pauperi,
    post te neque iratos trementi
        regum apices neque militum arma.

Te Liber et si laeta aderit Venus
segnesque nodum solvere Gratiae
    vivaeque producent lucernae,
        dum rediens fugat astra Phoebus.

Corvinus has called for a mellower wine, therefore,
O virtuous jar, born the same year as I,
In the consulship of Manlius, appear,
Descend, bring forth whatever there may be,

Laughter, or quarrelsomeness, sleepiness, or the complaints
Of dejected lovers, whatever it happens to be
The grapes were gathered for to make this Massic,
Matured to be just right for some special occasion.

Soaked in serious studies though he be,
Corvinus is not averse to the pleasure of wine.
Old Cato the stern and righteous, it's said, was accustomed
To use this pleasant means to warm himself up.

Your gentle discipline encourages
The dull to be less dull than usual,
And Bacchus, joyful Deliverer, reveals
What the sober wise man really meant to say.

You bring back hope to the despairing heart
And you give courage to the poor man, so
He's neither scared of tyrants in their crowns
Nor soldiers brandishing their scary weapons.

Bacchus attends thee, and Venus, if she's willing,
And torchlight, and the Graces dancing together,
Until the moment the returning sun
Puts all the stars to flight, and the party's over.

iii.22

Montium custos nemorumque, Virgo,
quae laborantis utero puellas
ter vocata audis adimisque leto,
    diva triformis,

imminens villae tua pinus esto,
quam per exactos ego laetus annos
verris obliquum meditantis ictum
    sanguine donem.

Virgin, goddess, goddess of the groves
And of the hills, goddess to whom the young
Mother in her labor cries out three times

And then again cries out three times O goddess,
Goddess, to hear and rescue her from death,
O goddess triple-formed, I dedicate

This pine tree by my dwelling-house to you,
And promise to offer every year the blood
Of a young boar just learning to use his tusks.

iii.23

Caelo supinas si tuleris manus
nascente luna, rustica Phidyle,
  si ture placaris et horna
    fruge Lares avidaque porca,

nec pestilentem sentiet Africum
fecunda vitis nec sterilem seges
  robiginem aut dulces alumni
    pomifero grave tempus anno.

Nam quae nivali pascitur Algido
devota quercus inter et ilices
  aut crescit Albanis in herbis
    victima, pontificum securis

cervice tinguet: te nihil attinet
temptare multa caede bidentium
  parvos coronantem marino
    rore deos fragilique myrto.

Phidyle, if you raise
  Your hands to pray when the new
    Moon rises up again

Or if you please the Lares
  With a little incense or
    With a simple garland made

From what you grew this year,
  Or with a suckling pig,
    Why then you need not fear

That the bad South Wind will harm
  Your vines or that the blight
    Will blight your grain or that

In the apple-bearing season
  The autumn sickness hurtful
    To beasts will hurt your flock.

Right now the foredoomed victim
  Whose blood will stain the ax
    In the costly priestly rites

Is grazing among the oaks
  And ilex on the side
    Of snowy Mount Algidus

Or else upon the grasses
  Of Mount Albanus; so
    You need not sacrifice

A full-grown sheep or other
  Costly offering.
    All you need to do

Is adorn your little home-made
  Images of the gods
    With rosemary and myrtle.

Immunis aram si tetigit manus,
non sumptuosa blandior hostia,
    mollivit aversos Penatis
        farre pio et saliente mica.

So long as the hands are pure
   The offering is made with,
      You need do nothing more

Than lay upon the fire
   An offering of meal
      And crackling country salt.

iii.24

Intactis opulentior
   thesauris Arabum et divitis Indiae
caementis licet occupes
   terrenum omne tuis et mare publicum,

si figit adamantinos
   summis verticibus dira Necessitas
clavos, non animum metu,
   non mortis laqueis expedies caput.

Campestres melius Scythae,
   quorum plaustra vagas rite trahunt domos,
vivunt et rigidi Getae,
   immetata quibus iugera liberas

fruges et Cererem ferunt,
   nec cultura placet longior annua,
defunctumque laboribus
   aequali recreat sorte vicarius.

Illic matre carentibus
   privignis mulier temperat innocens,
nec dotata regit virum
   coniunx nec nitido fidit adultero.

If the last nail driven in
   To finish off your roof
Is the adamantine nail
   That grim Necessity drives,

It simply doesn't matter
   However rich you are,
Not even supposing
   You had more riches than

Arabia has or than
   India has; not even
Supposing that your villa
   Encroached on most of the land

And out over the sea.
   You can't get rid of the fear.
You can't get loose from the trap
   Death has laid down for you.

The Scythians do it better:
   They move from place to place
With their houses on their wagons;
   The Getae do it better:

They share the land and share
   The produce of the land;
Each man has his tillage
   Only for a year,

Then another takes his turn.
   Among these rigorous people
The women nurse and cherish
   The little orphan children;

No maiden has a dower
   To use to lord it over
Her husband when she marries;
   Nor does her money tempt her

Dos est magna parentium
    virtus et metuens alterius viri
certo foedere castitas,
    et peccare nefas aut pretium est mori.

O quisquis volet impias
    caedes et rabiem tollere civicam,
si quaeret "Pater urbium"
    subscribi statuis, indomitam audeat

refrenare licentiam,
    clarus postgenitis: quatenus—heu nefas!—
virtutem incolumem odimus,
    sublatam ex oculis quaerimus invidi.

Quid tristes querimoniae,
    si non supplicio culpa reciditur;
quid leges sine moribus
    vanae proficiunt, si neque fervidis

To put herself in the power
	Of some meretricious lover.
Her dower is her virtue,
	Inherited from her parents,

Her chastity untempted
	By somebody else's husband.
They abhor wrongdoing there;
	The punishment is death.

Whoever wants to have it
	Written on his statue,
"He was his city's father,"
	And wants to do away

With civil war and bloodshed,
	He must restrain us from
Our talent for being vicious,
	And furthermore must settle

For not being thanked until
	He cannot hear our thanks,
Because, O shame of Rome,
	It seems that, in our envy,

We hate the good man while
	He's still alive, and then
We praise him when he's dead.
	What good does it do to say

We're sorry, we repent,
	If the shears of punishment
Don't cut away the evil?
	What good is in our laws

If they don't mean what they say?
	If there's no toughness in us
To see to it they do?
	What does it matter if

pars inclusa caloribus
    mundi nec Boreae finitimum latus
durataeque solo nives
    mercatorem abigunt, horrida callidi

vincunt aequora navitae,
    magnum pauperies opprobrium iubet
quidvis et facere et pati,
    virtutisque viam deserit arduae?

Vel nos in Capitolium,
    quo clamor vocat et turba faventium,
vel nos in mare proximum
    gemmas et lapides aurum et inutile,

summi materiem mali,
    mittamus, scelerum si bene paenitet.
Eradenda cupidinis
    pravi sunt elementa et tenerae nimis

mentes asperioribus
    formandae studiis. Nescit equo rudis
haerere ingenuus puer
    venarique timet, ludere doctior,

We go to the ends of the earth?
  What does it matter if
Neither the regions where
  The sands are burning hot

Nor the boreal regions where
  The ground is freezing cold
Can keep our traders out?
  What if our skillful sailors

Conquer the seas, what matter,
  If money, the lack of it
Being thought to be such a shame,
  Drives men to do or suffer

Anything whatsoever,
  If the path they take is not
The arduous path of virtue?
  If we really do repent,

Let us take all our jewels
  And all our useless gold
And all such precious things
  Up to the Capitoline

And throw them all away
  While the cheering crowd applauds,
Or let's pitch all such stuff,
  The material of our grief,

Into the nearest ocean.
  We must eradicate
The sources of our vices;
  Our frail souls must be trained

By harder exercises.
  The freeborn Roman youth
Is afraid to go out hunting;
  He doesn't even know how

seu Graeco iubeas trocho,
    seu malis vetita legibus alea,
cum periura patris fides
    consortem socium fallat et hospites

indignoque pecuniam
    heredi properet. Scilicet improbae
crescunt divitiae; tamen
    curtae nescio quid semper abest rei.

To keep his seat on a horse—
   But he knows very well
How to play at Grecian hoops,
   And even better how

To play the illegal dice-game.
   Meanwhile his perjured father
Breaks faith with his business partner,
   And swindles his best friends,

Busy making a fortune
   For his no-good son and heir.
The money grows and grows,
   But something's always lacking.

Quo me, Bacche, rapis tui
    plenum? Quae nemora aut quos agor in specus,
velox mente nova? Quibus
    antris egregii Caesaris audiar

aeternum meditans decus
    stellis inserere et consilio Iovis?
Dicam insigne, recens, adhuc
    indictum ore alio. Non secus in iugis

exsomnis stupet Euhias,
    Hebrum prospiciens et nive candidam
Thracen aut pede barbaro
    lustratam Rhodopen, ut mihi devio

ripas et vacuum nemus
    mirari libet. O Naïadum potens
Baccharumque valentium
    proceras manibus vertere fraxinos,

nil parvum aut humili modo,
    nil mortale loquar. Dulce periculum est,
o Lenaeë, sequi deum
    cingentem viridi tempora pampino.

iii.25 / *To Bacchus*

Where is it, where am I going to, Bacchus, where,
Where are you taking me, filled as I am with the god?

What are the grottoes? What are the groves, Oh where,
Where am I going to, altered in mind? Where, where,

What are the caves where the echoing sound of my music
Rehearses to celebrate Caesar, singing his glory

Among the stars in the sky and at Jupiter's table,
Singing the praise of Caesar's newest deed

As yet unsung by any other singer.
As when a sleepless lone Bacchante stands

Gazing across the ranges stupefied
At shining snowy Thrace and Hebrus there

And Rhodope almost untrodden on,
So, like the Bacchante, in amazement I

Transfixed stand gazing at the lonely groves
And riverbanks I wander near. O you,

Who rule the Naiads and the Bacchantes who
Uproot whole trees with their bare hands and hurl them,

I shall speak nothing mean or ordinary,
Nor what is only mortal. Joyful is

The fearfulness of following the god,
Wearing the vine-leaf garland as my sign.

Vixi puellis nuper idoneus
et militavi non sine gloria.
   nunc arma defunctumque bello
      barbiton hic paries habebit,

laevum marinae qui Veneris latus
custodit. Hic, hic ponite lucida
   funalia et vectes et arcus
      oppositis foribus minacis.

O quae beatam diva tenes Cyprum et
Memphin carentem Sithonia nive,
   regina, sublimi flagello
      tange Chloen semel arrogantem.

iii.26 / *To Venus*

Experienced in your wars,
Not long ago I was
A not inglorious soldier,
But now upon this wall,
Beside the effigy of
Venus, goddess of love,
Born from the glittering sea,

I place these weapons and
This lyre no longer fit
For use in the wars of love.
Here I offer the torch,
The crowbar and the bow,
Siege weapons used
Against those closed-up doors.

O goddess, queen of Cyprus,
Queen of sunny Memphis,
Far from the snows of Thrace,
All I ask of you
Is one punishing flick
Of your uplifted lash
To sting arrogant Chloë.

iii.27

Impios parrae recinentis omen
ducat et praegnans canis aut ab agro
rava recurrens lupa Lanuvino
    fetaque vulpes;

rumpat et serpens iter institutum,
si per obliquum similis sagittae
terruit mannos: ego cui timebo,
    providus auspex,

antequam stantis repetat paludes
imbrium divina avis imminentum,
oscinem corvum prece suscitabo
    solis ab ortu.

Sis licet felix, ubicumque mavis,
et memor nostri, Galatea, vivas;
teque nec laevus vetet ire picus
    nec vaga cornix.

Sed vides quanto trepidet tumultu
pronus Orion? Ego quid sit ater
Hadriae novi sinus et quid albus
    peccet Iapyx.

Hostium uxores puerique caecos
sentiant motus orientis Austri et
aequoris nigri fremitum et trementis
    verbere ripas.

Sic et Europe niveum doloso
credidit tauro latus et scatentem
beluïs pontum mediasque fraudes
    palluit audax.

Nuper in pratis studiosa florum et
debitae Nymphis opifex coronae,
nocte sublustri nihil astra praeter
    vidit et undas.

May bad people see bad omens everywhere,
The screech of an owl, the sight of a pregnant dog,
Or a gray she-wolf running across a field,
Or maybe a fox that's lately dropped her litter;

Or may they see a serpent like an arrow
Slither obliquely across, scaring the horses.
My prayers will make good omens for good people.
I'll look to the east and call upon the raven

To sing good fortune to come to those I fear for,
Before he has a chance to fly to the west,
To the standing pools, to prophesy bad weather.
Wherever it is your heart desires to go,

Go safely there and be happy, Galatea,
Remembering with pleasure how we were.
Let no sinister magpie say you nay
Nor any wandering crow forbid your journey.

But you can see the tumult in the sky
When angry Orion sets. You know how black
The Adriatic can be, and what can go wrong
Even when Iapyx the favoring West Wind blows.

Oh rather may our enemies' wives and children
Experience the unexpected gales
The South Wind brings upon them, the roaring of
The blackening waters, the sound of the pounding surf

Shaking the beaches. Thus it was for Europa,
Entrusting the safety of her snow-white body
To the not to be trusted bull when in the very
Moment of her departure she was aghast

At the midnight sea swarming with terrible monsters.
She who had only a moment before that been
A pupil of the flowers of the fields
And a weaver of the garlands of the nymphs,

Quae simul centum tetigit potentem
oppidis Creten, "Pater, o relictum
filiae nomen pietasque," dixit
    "victa furore!

Unde quo veni? Levis una mors est
virginum culpae. Vigilansne ploro
turpe commisum an vitiis carentem
    ludit imago

vana, quae porta fugiens eburna
somnium ducit? Meliusne fluctus
ire per longos fuit an recentis
    carpere flores?

Si quis infamem mihi nunc iuvencum
dedat iratae, lacerare ferro et
frangere enitar modo multum amati
    cornua monstri.

Impudens liqui patrios Penates,
impudens Orcum moror. O deorum
si quis haec audis, utinam inter errem
    nuda leones!

Antequam turpis macies decentis
occupet malas teneraeque sucus
defluat praedae, speciosa quaero
    pascere tigris.

'Vilis Europe,' pater urget absens,
'Quid mori cessas? Potes hac ab orno
pendulum zona bene te secuta
    laedere collum;

sive te rupes et acuta leto
saxa delectant, age, te procellae
crede veloci, nisi erile mavis
    carpere pensum

Now all she saw in the blackness of the night
Were the waves of the sea and the faint light of stars.
At last she found herself upon the shore
Of the mighty hundred-citied island of Crete

And cried out to her father, "Father, I,
Who left behind my name and daughterly duty,
What madness was it that came over me?
Where am I now? Where is it I have come from?

One death alone is too little for such as I—
Am I in my senses, deploring the deed I did?—
Or didn't I do it? Was it some empty phantom
That flew up through the ivory gate of lies?—

Which was it better to do? To do as I did,
To fly here through the darkness over the waves—
Or stay back there in the field, gathering flowers?—
If that young bull were here before me now

I'd strike into its hide with avenging steel
And break the horns I lately hung with flowers.
Shameless I left the gods of my father's house.
Shameless I wait for Orcus to take me away.

If there are any gods who listen to me,
While still my beauty remains, send me, naked,
Out among lions, let me be eaten by tigers,
Before these fresh cheeks wither." "Vilest Europa,"

The voice of her father says from far away,
"Why do you put off dying? There is a tree,
An ash tree, near, to hang yourself upon
With the silken sash you luckily brought with you.

Unless, that is, the jagged rocks that lie
At the bottom of yonder cliff would please you better.
If that is so, just give yourself to the wind,
A royal princess otherwise fated to be

regius sanguis dominaeque tradi
barbarae paelex.' " Aderat querenti
perfidum ridens Venus et remisso
    filius arcu.

Mox ubi lusit satis, "Abstineto"
dixit "irarum calidaeque rixae,
cum tibi invisus laceranda reddet
    cornua taurus.

Uxor invicti Iovis esse nescis:
mitte singultus, bene ferre magnam
disce fortunam; tua sectus orbis
    nomina ducet."

A slave handmaiden to some savage queen."
Europa wept. Quite suddenly, there stood Venus,
Heartlessly laughing and laughing, and with her her son,
With his bow unstrung; and when Venus had laughed enough

She said, "Dry up your tears and quell your rage
When the bull presents its horns for you to break.
Europa, you are the bride of Jupiter.
Learn how to bear your great good fortune, for

A region of the world is named for you."

iii.28

Festo quid potius die
  Neptuni faciam? Prome reconditum,
Lyde, strenua Caecubum
  munitaeque adhibe vim sapientiae.

Inclinare meridiem
  sentis ac, veluti stet volucris dies,
parcis deripere horreo
  cessantem Bibuli consulis amphoram.

Nos cantabimus invicem
  Neptunum et viridis Nereïdum comas;
tu curva recines lyra
  Latonam et celeris spicula Cynthiae;

summo carmine, quae Cnidon
  fulgentisque tenet Cycladas et Paphum
iunctis visit oloribus;
  dicetur merita Nox quoque nenia.

iii.28 / *To Lyde*

What could be better to do on Neptune's day?
Lyde, go fetch the Caecuban wine, and hurry.
Let's strike a blow for folly. The sun is setting,
And yet you tarry as if the hour stands still—

Bring out that jar of vintage wine from the cellar,
The one that dates from Bibulus' consulship.
We'll sing some songs together on the shore:
First I the one about the god of the sea

And the green-haired nymphs, the Nereids; then you,
In reply, will sing, accompanied by the lyre,
The hymn to Latona and fleet Diana, and fleet
Diana's arrows; and then the one about

Venus, the Queen of the shining Cyclades,
The Queen of Cnidos, and how she comes to visit
Cyprian Paphos, drawn by her yoke of swans.
—And then a song appropriate to the dark.

iii.29

Tyrrhena regum progenies, tibi
non ante verso lene merum cado
    cum flore, Maecenas, rosarum et
        pressa tuis balanus capillis

iamdudum apud me est: eripe te morae,
nec semper udum Tibur et Aefulae
    declive contempleris arvum et
        Telegoni iuga parricidae.

Fastidiosam desere copiam et
molem propinquam nubibus arduis,
    omitte mirari beatae
        fumum et opes strepitumque Romae.

Plerumque gratae divitibus vices
mundaeque parvo sub lare pauperum
    cenae sine aulaeis et ostro
        sollicitam explicuere frontem.

Iam clarus occultum Andromedae pater
ostendit ignem, iam Procyon furit
    et stella vesani Leonis
        sole dies referente siccos;

iam pastor umbras cum grege languido
rivumque fessus quaerit et horridi
    dumeta Silvani, caretque
        ripa vagis taciturna ventis.

Tu civitatem quis deceat status
curas et urbi sollicitus times
    quid Seres et regnata Cyro
        Bactra parent Tanaïsque discors.

Prudens futuri temporis exitum
caliginosa nocte premit deus,
    ridetque si mortalis ultra
        fas trepidat. Quod adest memento

Maecenas, descendant of many Tuscan kings,
There's a jar of excellent country wine at my house,
Unopened, pure, saved specially for you,
And garlands of roses, and oil of balsam, too,

To anoint your hair. When you come to visit me,
Give up, for a time, the pleasures of the rich
In the smoke and noise and excitement of the city.
Sometimes it is another kind of pleasure

For the rich man to pretend to be a poor man,
To sit at the poor man's table and share a meal
In the poor man's simple house. How by such means
Anxiety may be calmed in the peace and quiet

Of such a fantasy! Wild Leo burns
In the nighttime sky and the lesser Dog Star rages,
And Cepheus, the father of Andromeda,
Shows forth. It is the season when the sun

Brings back the days of drought and heat, the days
When the weary shepherd and his weary flock
Seek out the riverbank and the shade of the grove,
And not a breath of air stirs in the scene.

Your mind, I know, is occupied with what
Concerns such men as you about the state:
The things the Seres might be planning, or
The Bactrians, once ruled by Cyrus, or

The troublesome Scythian tribe on the river Don.
It is wise of the god to conceal in the dark of the future
Whatever it is that is going to come to pass.
The god is amused at our anxieties.

Take care of the things you need to take care of today.
Everything else is as if borne on the Tiber.
One day the river flows along as calm
And peaceful as can be, down to the sea,

componere aequus; cetera fluminis
ritu feruntur, nunc medio alveo
    cum pace delabentis Etruscum
    in mare, nunc lapides adesos

stirpesque raptas et pecus et domos
volventis una non sine montium
    clamore vicinaeque silvae,
    cum fera diluvies quietos

irritat amnis. Ille potens sui
laetusque deget cui licet in diem
    dixisse "Vixi: cras vel atra
    nube polum pater occupato

vel sole puro; non tamen irritum
quodcumque retro est efficiet, neque
    diffinget infectumque reddet
    quod fugiens semel hora vexit."

Fortuna saevo laeta negotio et
ludum insolentem ludere pertinax
    transmutat incertos honores,
    nunc mihi, nunc alii benigna.

Laudo manentem; si celeris quatit
pinnas, resigno quae dedit et mea
    virtute me involvo probamque
    pauperiem sine dote quaero.

Non est meum, si mugiat Africis
malus procellis, ad miseras preces
    decurrere et votis pacisci,
    ne Cypriae Tyriaeque merces

addant avaro divitias mari:
tunc me biremis praesidio scaphae
    tutum per Aegaeos tumultus
    aura feret geminusque Pollux.

The next day carrying with it rolling boulders
And huge torn-loose tree trunks, and drowning beasts
Pawing the flood, and houses swept away,
While all around the mountainsides and forests

Sound with the echoing noise of how the storm
Transformed the quiet stream from what it was.
Happy the man who has earned the right to say:
"I've lived my life. There may be storms tomorrow,

Maybe fair weather. Nobody knows for sure.
What I have had in the past cannot be taken
Away from me now. Fortune, who loves to play
Her cruel game and plays it over and over,

Can do what she likes with me or anyone else.
I'll praise her while she favors me, but when,
As she prepares to fly away, I hear
The rustling of her wings, I'll yield my luck

And wrap myself as in a garment in
My knowledge of who I am and what I've been,
And freely welcome honest Poverty,
Who has no gifts to give. Let the storm come on,

Let my little boat shudder and plunge in the turbulent sea,
I will not do as the voyaging merchant does
And cravenly pray and bargain with vows to the gods
To save my goods. I'll ride the storm out, and,

Perhaps, at last, with the help of the heavenly twins,
Castor and Pollux, under whose fortunate sign
The storm subsides and the clouds disperse, I'll sail,
Carried by clearing breezes, safe into port."

iii.30

Exegi monumentum aere perennius
regalique situ pyramidum altius,
quod non imber edax, non Aquilo impotens
possit diruere aut innumerabilis
annorum series et fuga temporum.
Non omnis moriar multaque pars mei
vitabit Libitinam; usque ego postera
crescam laude recens. Dum Capitolium
scandet cum tacita virgine pontifex,
dicar, qua violens obstrepit Aufidus
et qua pauper aquae Daunus agrestium
regnavit populorum, ex humili potens,
princeps Aeolium carmen ad Italos
deduxisse modos. Sume superbiam
quaesitam meritis et mihi Delphica
lauro cinge volens, Melpomene, comam.

iii.30

Today I have finished a work outlasting bronze
And the pyramids of ancient royal kings.
The North Wind raging cannot scatter it
Nor can the rain obliterate this work,
Nor can the years, nor can the ages passing.
Some part of me will live and not be given
Over into the hands of the death goddess.
I will go on and on, kept ever young
By the praise in times to come for what I have done.
So long as the Pontiff in solemn procession climbs
The Capitol steps, beside him the reverent Vestal,
So long will it be that men will say that I,
Born in a land where Aufidus' torrent roared,
Once ruled by Danaus, king of a peasant people,
Was the first to bring Aeolian measures to Latin.
Melpomene, look kindly on the honor
The Muse has won for me, and graciously
Place on my head the garland of Delphic laurel.

BOOK FOUR

Intermissa, Venus, diu
    rursus bella moves? Parce, precor, precor.
Non sum qualis eram bonae
    sub regno Cinarae. Desine, dulcium

mater saeva Cupidinum,
    circa lustra decem flectere mollibus
iam durum imperiis: abi,
    quo blandae iuvenum te revocant preces.

Tempestivius in domum
    Pauli, purpureis ales oloribus,
comissabere Maximi,
    si torrere iecur quaeris idoneum.

Namque et nobilis et decens
    et pro sollicitis non tacitus reis
et centum puer artium
    late signa feret militiae tuae;

et quandoque potentior
    largi muneribus riserit aemuli,
Albanos prope te lacus
    ponet marmoream sub trabe citrea.

Illic plurima naribus
    duces tura, lyraeque et Berecyntiae
delectabere tibiae
    mixtis carminibus non sine fistula;

illic bis pueri die
    numen cum teneris virginibus tuum
laudantes pede candido
    in morem Salium ter quatient humum.

Venus, it seems that now
   Your wars are starting again.
Spare me, spare me, I pray.
   I am not what I was
When tender Cynara ruled me.
   Spare me, O pitiless mother
Of all the amorini,
   For I am almost fifty.
Why don't you go to where
   You can hear the young men praying,
Praising you in their prayers?
   More exactly, if you seek
The most suitable heart to inflame,
   Why don't you go to the house,
Borne there by your swans,
   Of Paulus Maximus,
Good-looking, noble of mind,
   Defender of those to whom
Injustices have been done?
   He will carry your battle flag
Triumphantly in the field,
   And when he's won out easily
Over some spendthrift rival,
   He'll laugh in delight and he'll
Put up your statue in marble,
   By the side of the Alban lake,
Under an arbor of cedar.
   Your nostrils will inhale
Sweetest odors of incense
   And you will hear the music
Of the Berecynthian flute
   Accompanied by the lyre
And by the shepherd's pipe.
   Twice every day there'll be
Boys and tender maidens
   Dancing in honor of you,
Tripping with snow-white feet
   In the triple-time Salian way.
Now neither boys nor girls

Me nec femina nec puer
   iam nec spes animi credula mutui
nec certare iuvat mero
   nec vincire novis tempora floribus.

Sed cur heu, Ligurine, cur
   manat rara meas lacrima per genas?
Cur facunda parum decoro
   inter verba cadit lingua silentio?

Nocturnis ego somniis
   iam captum teneo, iam volucrem sequor
te per gramina Martii
   campi, te per aquas, dure, volubilis.

Delight me anymore,
Nor credulous hopes of love,
   Nor drinking bouts nor garlands
Woven of new spring flowers.
   But why, Ligurinus, why,
Every once in a while
   Do my eyes fill up with tears?
Why sometimes when I'm talking
   Do I suddenly fall silent?
I hold you fast, sometimes,
   Sometimes, at night, in a dream,
Or I follow you as you flee
   Across the Campus Martius,
O hard of heart, Ligurinus,
   Or as you are lost among
The bewildering waves of the river.

iv.2

Pindarum quisquis studet aemulari,
Iulle, ceratis ope Daedalea
nititur pinnis vitreo daturus
    nomina ponto.

Monte decurrens velut amnis, imbres
quem super notas aluere ripas,
fervet immensusque ruit profundo
    Pindarus ore,

laurea donandus Apollinari,
seu per audacis nova dithyrambos
verba devolvit numerisque fertur
    lege solutis,

seu deos regesque canit, deorum
sanguinem, per quos cecidere iusta
morte Centauri, cecidit tremendae
    flamma Chimaerae,

sive quos Eleä domum reducit
palma caelestis pugilemve equumve
dicit et centum potiore signis
    munere donat,

flebili sponsae iuvenemve raptum
plorat et viris animumque moresque
aureos educit in astra nigroque
    invidet Orco.

Multa Dircaeum levat aura cycnum,
tendit, Antoni, quotiens in altos
nubium tractus. Ego apis Matinae
    more modoque

iv.2 / *To Iullus Antonius*

Whoever seeks to emulate Pindar's music
   Takes flight on wings whose waxen fastenings
      Daedalus might have thought of; like Icarus he

Will leave his name on the waters of some sea.
   Pindar is like a river which the rain
      Has caused to rise above its proper banks

And overflowing rushes down the mountain
   Boiling and roaring; so the deep voice of Pindar
      Boils and roars and overflows its banks,

Apollo-favored torrent rushing down
   The mountainside of song, telling over and over
      In dithyrambic freedom how the gods

And kings who were the sons of gods brought down
   The Centaurs to their fate, and telling how
      The great Chimera monster's fiery breath

Was finally snuffed out, and telling how,
   After the famous games, the winners' names
      Were shouted to the sky as home they came—

The riders, the wrestlers, and the charioteers,
   The horses, the runners, and the discus throwers—
      More glory given to them by Pindar's voice

Than by a hundred statues standing mute
   Around the applauding city; and telling how,
      Leaving his bride bereft, the hero died

Alas too soon; and telling the listening stars
   The praises of that hero's shining virtue,
      Begrudging him to Orcus' dark embrace.

When the Dircean swan thus takes his rapturous flight
   He's carried up by music flying high
      As the highest clouds are high. Antonius, I

grata carpentis thyma per laborem
plurimum circa nemus uvidique
Tiburis ripas operosa parvus
    carmina fingo.

Concines maiore poeta plectro
Caesarem, quandoque trahet ferocis
per sacrum clivum merita decorus
    fronde Sygambros;

quo nihil maius meliusve terris
fata donavere bonique divi,
nec dabunt, quamvis redeant in aurum
    tempora priscum.

Concines laetosque dies et urbis
publicum ludum super impetrato
fortis Augusti reditu forumque
    litibus orbum.

Tum meae, si quid loquar audiendum,
vocis accedet bona pars, et "O sol
pulcher, o laudande!" canam, recepto
    Caesare felix.

Teque dum procedis, "io Triumphe!"
non semel dicemus, "io Triumphe!"
civitas omnis dabimusque divis
    tura benignis.

Te decem tauri totidemque vaccae,
me tener solvet vitulus, relicta
matre qui largis iuvenescit herbis
    in mea vota,

fronte curvatos imitatus ignis
tertium lunae referentis ortum,
qua notam duxit niveus videri,
    cetera fulvus.

Am like the humble bee, painstakingly
    Seeking to find the honey in the thyme
        That grows in lowly fragrant groves and grows

Along the watery banks of Tivoli's stream;
    My songs are made laboriously and slow.
        But you are fit to sing of Caesar's triumph

Coming along the joyous Via Sacra,
    Behind him straggling the abject subject tribe—
        Caesar, than whom the fates and gods have given

No greater gift to the world, nor shall they give
    A greater gift, not even if this age
        Were once again to be the Golden Age.

Thus, Antonius, you will sing of the day
    Of festive games for Caesar's coming home
        As we had prayed for. As the procession passes,

My voice will be among the elated voices
    Crying out with the others in the crowd,
        "O joyful day!" as you pass by in the vanguard.

"Io Triumphe!" will the cry be heard,
    "Io Triumphe!" will be heard as we
        Bring offerings to celebrate the day.

Antonius, what you bring in song will be
    An offering of ten fine bulls and also
        Of ten fine cows; my offering's but a calf,

Recently weaned, cropping the grass in the pasture,
    Just parted from its mother; its little horns
        Are crescent-curved, exactly the way the moon,

The third night after you first can see it, looks.
    This little calf is tawny in color mostly,
        But with a white patch, white as the whitest snow.

iv.3

Quem tu, Melpomene, semel
  nascentem placido lumine videris,
illum non labor Isthmius
  clarabit pugilem, non equus impiger

curru ducet Achaïco
  victorem, neque res bellica Deliis
ornatum foliis ducem,
  quod regum tumidas contuderit minas,

ostendet Capitolio:
  sed quae Tibur aquae fertile praefluunt
et spissae nemorum comae
  fingent Aeolio carmine nobilem.

Romae, principis urbium,
  dignatur suboles inter amabilis
vatum ponere me choros,
  et iam dente minus mordeor invido.

O testudinis aureae
  dulcem quae strepitum, Pieri, temperas,
o mutis quoque piscibus
  donatura cycni, si libeat, sonum,

He whom you looked upon,
  Melpomene, at his birth,
With gentle approving eyes,
  Sitting beside his cradle,
Will not be drawn in triumph
  In the festive Achaean car,
Victor in games, nor will
  Long practice in the skill
Make him a famous boxer;
  Nor at the Capitol,
Returning from a war
  With Delian garlands crowned
And drawn by nodding horses,
  Will crowds applaud how he
Defeated haughty kings.
  No, the nurturing waters
That flow past Tibur's fields
  And Tibur's leafy groves
Shall bring him to fame for those
  Aeolian songs he sang.

Apparently the children
  Of Rome, the queen of cities,
Grant me their approbation
  To sing among the poets;
Now I feel less often
  How envy's tooth can bite.
Melpomene, O Muse,
  Knowing how to adjust
And regulate to sweetness
  The notes of the golden shell,
You could, if you so chose,
  Instruct the silent fish
To sing as well as the swan.
  It is entirely by
Your favoring gift that others,
  Seeing me on the street,

totum muneris hoc tui est,
  quod monstror digito praetereuntium
Romanae fidicen lyrae;
  quod spiro et placeo, si placeo, tuum est.

Point me out as he
   Who plays the Roman lute;
It is your gift if I
   Should please, if I do please.

iv.4

Qualem ministrum fulminis alitem,
cui rex deorum regnum in avis vagas
   permisit, expertus fidelem
      Iuppiter in Ganymede flavo,

olim iuventas et patrius vigor
nido laborum propulit inscium,
   vernique iam nimbis remotis
      insolitos docuere nisus

venti paventem, mox in ovilia
demisit hostem vividus impetus,
   nunc in reluctantis dracones
      egit amor dapis atque pugnae;

qualemve laetis caprea pascuis
intenta fulvae matris ab ubere
   iam lacte depulsum leonem
      dente novo peritura vidit,

videre Raetis bella sub Alpibus
Drusum gerentem Vindelici (quibus
   mos unde deductus per omne
      tempus Amazonia securi

dextras obarmet, quaerere distuli,
nec scire fas est omnia), sed diu
   lateque victrices catervae
      consiliis iuvenis revictae

sensere quid mens rite, quid indoles
nutrita faustis sub penetralibus
   posset, quid Augusti paternus
      in pueros animus Nerones.

Fortes creantur fortibus et bonis;
est in iuvencis, est in equis patrum
   virtus, neque imbellem feroces
      progenerant aquilae columbam.

Just as the winged minister of the lightning,
Whom the king of the gods made king of all the birds
(Having learned to trust him when he carried up
From earth to heaven the yellow-haired Ganymede),

Just as this eagle, when he was still an eaglet,
Impelled by youth and daring, ventured forth
Out of the nest, fearful and ignorant,
Not knowing yet what eagles do to be eagles,

Soon was instructed on the vernal winds,
The worst of the storms of winter being past,
How to do his eagle best, and soon he dove
Eagerly down on a sheepfold, and after that,

Hungry for prey and loving it he swoops
Down on the struggling serpents meant for him;
—Or, just as a doe, having discovered a meadow
That promises rich grazing, sees a young lion

Freshly weaned from his tawny mother's milk,
And sees that she is doomed to his young teeth—
The Vindelici saw young Drusus as
He harried the foe beneath the Rhaetian Alps.

I do not know nor do I seek to know
Where the custom came from, that since time began
Vindelici warriors have always carried
The Amazonian ax in their right hands;

But these formidable fighters soon came to know
What this young hero's wisdom was, and learned
What he could do, his power of mind and heart,
Nourished in the imperial house he came from,

And they were made to feel the enabling power
Of Augustus' paternal care for the two young Neros.
The strong and brave come from the strong and brave.
In steers, in horses, breeding shows itself;

Doctrina sed vim promovet insitam,
rectique cultus pectora roborant;
　　utcumque defecere mores,
　　　　indecorant bene nata culpae.

Quid debeas, o Roma, Neronibus,
testis Metaurum flumen et Hasdrubal
　　devictus et pulcher fugatis
　　　　ille dies Latio tenebris,

qui primus alma risit adorea,
dirus per urbes Afer ut Italas
　　ceu flamma per taedas vel Eurus
　　　　per Siculas equitavit undas.

Post hoc secundis usque laboribus
Romana pubes crevit, et impio
　　vastata Poenorum tumultu
　　　　fana deos habuere rectos,

dixitque tandem perfidus Hannibal:
"Cervi luporum praeda rapacium,
　　sectamur ultro quos opimus
　　　　fallere et effugere est triumphus.

Gens, quae cremato fortis ab Ilio
iactata Tuscis aequoribus sacra
　　natosque maturosque patres
　　　　pertulit Ausonias ad urbes,

duris ut ilex tonsa bipennibus
nigrae feraci frondis in Algido,
　　per damna, per caedes ab ipso
　　　　ducit opes animumque ferro.

Non hydra secto corpore firmior
vinci dolentem crevit in Herculem,
　　monstrumve submisere Colchi
　　　　maius Echioniaeve Thebae.

Nor do fierce eagles sire peace-loving doves.
But discipline improves on what is given;
Active pursuit of the good strengthens the heart;
Failure of will can ruin the richly gifted.

O Rome, the Metaurus River tells the story
Of what Rome owes the Nero family,
And fallen Hasdrubal tells, and that beautiful day
When the shadows fled from Latium, that beautiful day

Of the realization of victory over the dreadful
African who made his ruinous way
Through the towns of Italy, as in a forest
A fire will make its way through the tops of trees

Or as a storm wind races across the waves.
From that day on the Roman forces grew stronger
And the gods the impious Carthaginian toppled
Were restored once more to their proper Roman shrines.

Then treacherous Hannibal said, "We are like deer,
The natural prey of fearsome ravening wolves;
We are foolishly stalking after that which will eat us.
It would have been better to flee and baffle them.

These Romans rose from the ashes of burning Troy
And picked up their gods, their children, and their fathers,
And carried them over the dangerous Tuscan seas
And settled them down as if they had brought them home.

They're like an oak on the great dark forested side
Of Mount Algidus, shorn of a leafy limb
By the stroke of a two-edged ax; it nevertheless
Grows stronger still, as if by the force of the blow.

The Hydra, when its body was cut in pieces
Grew stronger still, unwilling to die; it wasn't
Stronger than these Romans are; the soldiers
Who sprang from the ground where the dragon's teeth were sown

Merses profundo, pulchrior evenit;
luctere, multa proruet integrum
 cum laude victorem geretque
  proelia coniugibus loquenda.

Carthagini iam non ego nuntios
mittam superbos; occidit, occidit
 spes omnis et fortuna nostri
  nominis Hasdrubale interempto."

Nil Claudiae non perficient manus,
quas et benigno numine Iuppiter
 defendit et curae sagaces
  expediunt per acuta belli.

Weren't more of a prodigy than prodigious Rome.
Drown it, it rises refreshed from the watery depths.
Let it be challenged to wrestle, it will bring down
The unrivaled champion, the victory something for women

To talk of with amazement for years to come.
I won't be sending exultant messages home
To Carthage anymore. All hope is lost,
Our reputation lost since Hasdrubal fell.

Now the Claudian house is entirely free
To do whatever it wants, and Jupiter
With radiant approval guards its fortunes.
They are guided by wisdom through the worst of wars."

Divis orte bonis, optime Romulae
custos gentis, abes iam nimium diu;
maturum reditum pollicitus patrum
    sancto concilio redi.

Lucem redde tuae, dux bone, patriae;
instar veris enim vultus ubi tuus
adfulsit populo, gratior it dies
    et soles melius nitent.

Ut mater iuvenem, quem Notus invido
flatu Carpathii trans maris aequora
cunctantem spatio longius annuo
    dulci distinet a domo,

votis ominibusque et precibus vocat,
curvo nec faciem litore dimovet:
sic desideriis icta fidelibus
    quaerit patria Caesarem.

Tutus bos etenim rura perambulat,
nutrit rura Ceres almaque Faustitas,
pacatum volitant per mare navitae;
    culpari metuit fides,

nullis polluitur casta domus stupris,
mos et lex maculosum edomuit nefas,
laudantur simili prole puerperae,
    culpam poena premit comes.

Quis Parthum paveat, quis gelidum Scythen,
quis Germania quos horrida parturit
fetus, incolumi Caesare? Quis ferae
    bellum curet Hiberiae?

Condit quisque diem collibus in suis,
et vitem viduas ducit ad arbores;
hinc ad vina redit laetus et alteris
    te mensis adhibet deum;

Custodian of the people who descend
From Romulus, the grandsire and the founder
Of the city you have promised to return to,
O blessèd guardian, shine upon your country,

For then the Roman day will be more pleasant,
The sunlight brighter, then it will be like spring.
Rome longs for Caesar's return the way a mother
Longs for her son's return to his parents' home.

Day after day she stands upon the shore;
She prays, and utters vows, and tries to read
The omens of the weather and the gods;
She never turns her face away from the sea.

When Caesar is here, the oxen peacefully browse
Across their pastures; Prosperity and Ceres
Nurture the crops; the dangerous seas are safe;
Faith shuns corruption; the private home is chaste—

Both custom and law see to it that it is so;
Mothers are praised for the likeness of virtuous sons
To virtuous fathers; punishment for a crime
Is sure to come hard on the heels of the crime's commission.

While Caesar lives who fears the Parthians?
Or the outcome of the war over in Spain?
Who fears the ice-cold Scythians? Who fears
The threatening bearded tribes of Germany?

Men go about the business of their vineyards,
Peacefully training their vines to marry their trees;
Then as the sun goes down they go to their houses
And to their suppers, and at the second course,

At the libation time, they offer up
Their prayers to you as to their household gods,
Just as the Grecians used to offer up
Their prayers to Castor and to Hercules.

te multa prece, te prosequitur mero
defuso pateris, et Laribus tuum
miscet numen, uti Graecia Castoris
    et magni memor Herculis.

"Longas o utinam, dux bone, ferias
praestes Hesperiae!" dicimus integro
sicci mane die, dicimus uvidi,
    cum sol Oceano subest.

"O blessèd guardian, grant that there may be
Long-lasting holiday for Italy."
Thus the prayer we make when the day begins;
Thus with our wine we pray when the sun goes down.

iv.6

Dive, quem proles Niobaea magnae
vindicem linguae Tityosque raptor
sensit et Troiae prope victor altae
    Phthius Achilles,

ceteris maior, tibi miles impar,
filius quamvis Thetidis marinae
Dardanas turris quateret tremenda
    cuspide pugnax—

ille, mordaci velut icta ferro
pinus aut impulsa cupressus Euro,
procidit late posuitque collum in
    pulvere Teucro.

Ille non inclusus equo Minervae
sacra mentito male feriatos
Troas et laetam Priami choreis
    falleret aulam,

sed palam captis gravis, heu nefas! heu!
nescios fari pueros Achivis
ureret flammis, etiam latentem
    matris in alvo,

ni tuis flexus Venerisque gratae
vocibus divum pater adnuisset
rebus Aeneae potiore ductos
    alite muros.

Doctor argutae fidicen Thaliae,
Phoebe, qui Xantho lavis amne crinis,
Dauniae defende decus Camenae,
    levis Agyieu.

iv.6 / *To Apollo*

Mighty Apollo, Latona's son, your rage
Taught Niobe's dying children how to pay
For Niobe's motherly boasting, and your rage
    Taught Tityos in Hades

The price for his offense against Latona.
Achilles came to know it, too, when almost
Having achieved the victory over Troy,
    Achilles, the son of Thetis—

Achilles who shook the towers because of the deeds
Of his spear that loved the battle with such passion,
Achilles stronger than others but nothing like
    A match for you, Apollo—

Fell like a pine tree when the ax has struck it
Or like a cypress brought down by the wind.
He lay full length and ate the dust of Troy.
    Achilles never would

Have hidden himself within the horse, the Trick,
Sent in while the Trojans danced in celebration.
Achilles would have come (alas! the horror!)
    In honest fury raging,

Putting into the fire the little children
Unable yet to speak, not sparing even
The unborn in the womb, if Jupiter hadn't
    Listened to Apollo

And listened to the pleas of charming Venus,
And so been brought to promise to Aeneas
And promise to his descendants luckier walls
    Than those of fallen Troy.

O Phoebus Apollo, divine musician, teacher
Who taught the melodious Muse her music, you
Who bathed in Xanthus' stream, beardless Agyieus,
    Protector of the city,

Spiritum Phoebus mihi, Phoebus artem
carminis nomenque dedit poetae.
Virginum primae puerique claris
    patribus orti,

Deliae tutela deae, fugacis
lyncas et cervos cohibentis arcu,
Lesbium servate pedem meique
    pollicis ictum,

rite Latonae puerum canentes,
rite crescentem face Noctilucam,
prosperam frugum celeremque pronos
    volvere mensis.

Nupta iam dices "Ego dis amicum,
saeculo festas referente luces,
reddidi carmen docilis modorum
    vatis Horati."

Befriend me now and my Apulian Muse,
Phoebus Apollo who taught me the rules of the art
And gave me the name of poet. You excellent children
    Of excellent fathers, wards

Of Diana the huntress, whose arrow never fails
To slay the lynx and roebuck as they flee,
Observe the measure I keep to my finger's beat
    As you sing the ritual hymn

To Latona's son and Diana the light of the moon
That prospers the crops as they grow and governs the months
Of the year in their regular turning. The bride, someday,
    On her wedding day, will say:

"Ten times eleven years brought round the time
To sing the saecular hymn to please the gods
And I was one of the children chosen to sing,
    Taught by the poet Horace."

iv.7

Diffugere nives, redeunt iam gramina campis
    arboribusque comae;
mutat terra vices et decrescentia ripas
    flumina praetereunt;

Gratia cum Nymphis geminisque sororibus audet
    ducere nuda choros.
Immortalia ne speres, monet annus et almum
    quae rapit hora diem.

Frigora mitescunt zephyris, ver proterit aestas,
    interitura simul
pomifer autumnus fruges effuderit, et mox
    bruma recurrit iners.

Damna tamen celeres reparant caelestia lunae;
    nos ubi decidimus
quo pius Aeneas, quo Tullus dives et Ancus,
    pulvis et umbra sumus.

Quis scit an adiciant hodiernae crastina summae
    tempora di superi?
Cuncta manus avidas fugient heredis, amico
    quae dederis animo.

Cum semel occideris et de te splendida Minos
    fecerit arbitria,
non, Torquate, genus, non te facundia, non te
    restituet pietas;

infernis neque enim tenebris Diana pudicum
    liberat Hippolytum,
nec Lethaea valet Theseus abrumpere caro
    vincula Pirithoö.

Now at last the snow has gone away;
The grass is beginning to show itself in the fields;
The leaves are just coming out on the springtime branches;
The changing earth is changing once again;
The rivers are running more easily past their banks,
And soon the Nymphs and soon the sister Graces
Will dare to dance unclothed in the springtime meadow.
Torquatus, don't pin your hopes on living forever.

The changing year gives you fair warning not to;
So does the hour that takes away the daylight;
Winter's cold air melts into the warmth of spring;
Then spring is trampled down under the summer;
Summer is buried under the apples of autumn;
And winter comes back in with its ice and cold.
Yet after a time, and time and time again,
The moon restores itself in the nighttime sky.

But when it's time for us to go down there
Where Aeneas went, the pious, and Tullus the rich,
And old King Ancus Martius, and all the others,
Then we're nothing but dust, we're nothing but shadows.
Who knows whether tomorrow the gods will have
Anything more to give than they have given?
What you can give to your own dear heart today
Will not fall into the clutch of your heir tomorrow.

Torquatus, once you've died and Minos the judge
Has spoken his words down there, then neither rank
Nor eloquence nor virtue—none of these—
Can ever bring you back to life again.
Diana herself is unable to free the shade
Of chaste Hippolytus, though he was chaste;
Theseus cannot break the chains of Lethe
To free his beloved Pirithous from the dark.

iv.8

Donarem pateras grataque commodus,
Censorine, meis aera sodalibus,
donarem tripodas, praemia fortium
Graiorum, neque tu pessima munerum
ferres, divite me scilicet artium,
quas aut Parrhasius protulit aut Scopas,
hic saxo, liquidis ille coloribus
sollers nunc hominem ponere, nunc deum.
Sed non haec mihi vis, non tibi talium
res est aut animus deliciarum egens.
Gaudes carminibus; carmina possumus
donare et pretium dicere muneri.
Non incisa notis marmora publicis,
per quae spiritus et vita redit bonis
post mortem ducibus, non celeres fugae
reiectaeque retrorsum Hannibalis minae,
non incendia Carthaginis impiae
eius, qui domita nomen ab Africa
lucratus rediit, clarius indicant
laudes quam Calabrae Pierides; neque
si chartae sileant quod bene feceris,
mercedem tuleris. Quid foret Iliae
Mavortisque puer, si taciturnitas
obstaret meritis invida Romuli?
Ereptum Stygiis fluctibus Aeacum
virtus et favor et lingua potentium
vatum divitibus consecrat insulis.

iv.8 / *To Censorinus*

If I had plenty of money, Censorinus,
   I could give other kinds
      Of presents to my friends,

Bowls, and bronzes, and tripods, antique Greek treasures,
   Things painted by Parrhasius,
      Or things that Scopas sculpted,

Skillfully representing gods or heroes.
   And you would by no means have
      The least of these. But I

Don't have the power to give any such gifts,
   Nor do you need such trifles.
      It is poetry you love.

It is poetry I can give, and I know its worth.
   Marble can tell the story
      Of what the dead hero did

Bringing him back to life engraved in stone,
   Of how Hannibal fled,
      His threats on his own head,

And how Scipio by his African conquest came
   Home with a new name;
      But stone cannot tell as well

As poetry can the tale; nor would you have
   The praise you merit if
      Your story went unwritten.

Who would Romulus be, the son of Ilia
   And the son of Mars, had silence,
      Envious of his deeds,

Held back the telling? And who was it who rescued
   Aeacus from the Stygian
      Waters of oblivion

Dignum laude virum Musa vetat mori:
caelo Musa beat. Sic Iovis interest
optatis epulis impiger Hercules,
clarum Tyndaridae sidus ab infimis
quassas eripiunt aequoribus rates,
ornatus viridi tempora pampino
Liber vota bonos ducit ad exitus.

And brought him safe ashore on the Blessèd Isle?
    It was poetry rescued him.
        Poetry forbids

That he who deserves our praise will be forgotten.
    The blessing of the Muse
        Is on the hero's head.

Thus Hercules, an honored guest, is welcome
    At Jupiter's banquet table;
        And the shining stars, the brothers

Castor and Pollux, quiet the waters, and
    The storm-stricken vessel
        Makes it home to port;

And over the woodland festival Bacchus presides,
    Wearing his crown of ivy,
        All promises having been kept.

Ne forte credas interitura quae
longe sonantem natus ad Aufidum
    non ante vulgatas per artis
        verba loquor socianda chordis,

non, si priores Maeonius tenet
sedes Homerus, Pindaricae latent
    Ceaeque et Alcaei minaces
        Stesichorive graves Camenae;

nec si quid olim lusit Anacreon
delevit aetas; spirat adhuc amor
    vivuntque commissi calores
        Aeoliae fidibus puellae.

Non sola comptos arsit adulteri
crinis et aurum vestibus illitum
    mirata regalisque cultus
        et comites Helene Lacaena,

primusve Teucer tela Cydonio
direxit arcu; non semel Ilios
    vexata; non pugnavit ingens
        Idomeneus Sthenelusve solus

dicenda Musis proelia; non ferox
Hector vel acer Deïphobus gravis
    excepit ictus pro pudicis
        coniugibus puerisque primus.

Vixere fortes ante Agamemnona
multi; sed omnes illacrimabiles
    urgentur ignotique longa
        nocte, carent quia vate sacro.

Paulum sepultae distat inertiae
celata virtus. Non ego te meis
    chartis inornatum silebo,
        totve tuos patiar labores

Do not believe these words will die away
Which I, born hearing the sound of my native river,
Speak in a music never known before,
    Accompanied by the lyre.

Homer, of course, is first among the poets,
But Pindar is not unpraised, Simonides
Is praised, Alcaeus the tyrant-hater, and grave
    Stesichorus of Himera.

The years have not erased from memory
The songs Anacreon played for his amusement;
And Sappho's passion lives and breathes confided
    To the strings of Sappho's lyre.

Helen was not the first to burn with love
Because of someone's adulterous elegant hairdo,
His wonderful gold-worked clothes, his retinue
    Of Oriental servants.

Teucer wasn't the first to draw the bow;
More Troys have been besieged than Troy itself;
Idomeneus and Sthenelus weren't the only
    Heroes to fight so well

The Muses should have sung about it; sturdy
Deiphobus and warlike Hector weren't
The only husbands and fathers to suffer blows
    Defending their wives and children.

Heroes have lived before Agamemnon lived,
But all of them are lost somewhere in the night,
Unwept, unknown, unless they had a poet
    To tell what was their story.

It's hard to know true worth from its opposite
When both are in the tomb. But, Lollius,
My lines will not be silent about your deeds.
    Spiteful forgetfulness

impune, Lolli, carpere lividas
obliviones. Est animus tibi
   rerumque prudens et secundis
      temporibus dubiisque rectus,

vindex avarae fraudis et abstinens
ducentis ad se cuncta pecuniae,
   consulque non unius anni,
      sed quotiens bonus atque fidus

iudex honestum praetulit utili,
reiecit alto dona nocentium
   vultu, per obstantis catervas
      explicuit sua victor arma.

Non possidentem multa vocaveris
recte beatum; rectius occupat
   nomen beati, qui deorum
      muneribus sapienter uti

duramve callet pauperiem pati
peiusque leto flagitium timet,
   non ille pro caris amicis
      aut patria timidus perire.

Will never be allowed to eat away
The memory of your honor. You have a mind
That knows the way things are and also knows
   The way things ought to be;

Resolute in the right, whether the times
Are good or bad; implacable enemy
Of fraud and greed; free of the spell of money
   That draws all to itself

The way a lodestone does; Lollius, you
Are consul not for one year only but
Whenever it is a virtuous judge is called for,
   One who prefers what's honest

To what's expedient, contemptuously
Disdaining the gifts corruption loves to offer.
You bear your honor as if you were bearing arms
   Against the opposing foe.

It isn't the man who owns a great many things
Who's rightly called blessed; that man is blessed who knows
What it means to make a proper use of the gifts
   The gods have given, and knows

What hardship is and how it is to be borne;
Who's more afraid of shame than he is of death,
And who's not afraid to give his life for his friends,
   Or for his native country.

O crudelis adhuc et Veneris muneribus potens,
insperata tuae cum veniet pluma superbiae
et quae nunc umeris involitant deciderint comae,
nunc et qui color est puniceae flore prior rosae
mutatus, Ligurine, in faciem verterit hispidam:
dices "Heu," quotiens te speculo videris alterum,
"quae mens est hodie, cur eadem non puero fuit,
vel cur his animis incolumes non redeunt genae?"

Still cruel and still endowed with power to be so,
Gifted as you are with the gifts of Venus,
That moment is coming, when, suddenly, in the glass,
You see beginning the little signs of change,
Downy foreshadowing of the beard to come,
The locks that curl and wanton to the shoulders
All of a sudden looking a little different,
The cream-and-rose complexion beyond the beauty
Of freshest roses now not quite exactly
The way it had been just yesterday morning.
Then you will say, Alas for what I was
When I was younger than I am, Alas
That then I did not know what I know now;
Alas, that now I know what I did not know.

Est mihi nonum superantis annum
plenus Albani cadus; est in horto,
Phylli, nectendis apium coronis;
    est hederae vis

multa, qua crinis religata fulges;
ridet argento domus; ara castis
vincta verbenis avet immolato
    spargier agno;

cuncta festinat manus, huc et illuc
cursitant mixtae pueris puellae;
sordidum flammae trepidant rotantes
    vertice fumum.

Ut tamen noris quibus advoceris
gaudiis, Idus tibi sunt agendae,
qui dies mensem Veneris marinae
    findit Aprilem,

iure sollemnis mihi sanctiorque
paene natali proprio, quod ex hac
luce Maecenas meus adfluentis
    ordinat annos.

Telephum, quem tu petis, occupavit
non tuae sortis iuvenem puella
dives et lasciva, tenetque grata
    compede vinctum.

Terret ambustus Phaëthon avaras
spes, et exemplum grave praebet ales
Pegasus terrenum equitem gravatus
    Bellerophontem,

semper ut te digna sequare et ultra
quam licet sperare nefas putando
disparem vites. Age iam, meorum
    finis amorum,

I have saved for the day a full bottle of old
Wine from the Alban hills. Phyllis, out in the garden
There's parsley, and ivy, for fillets and coronets
To bind up your hair and make you look still more
Beautiful than you looked even before.

The household is getting ready; the silver is polished,
The cups and flagons gleam; the household altar,
Adorned with leaves, is ready, awaiting the offerings.
Everyone hurries. The servants, the boys and girls,
Going this way and that, getting everything ready.
The air is alive with the smoke of fiery wreaths.

Today is the Ides of April, the month of Venus,
A festival day for me because of Maecenas,
Who celebrates today his natal day,
The onward flowing of another year.

I have to tell you something. Telephus,
The highborn boy you love, loves somebody else.
She's wanton, young, and rich; he's fettered to her
By chains of delight. Scorched Phaëthon flew too high,
And wingèd Pegasus flying toward heaven shook
The burden of Bellerophon from his back.
There is a lesson in this. Learn from example.

Love only as it is fitting; do not desire
That which you ought not to have. Phyllis, listen to me:
You are the last of my loves; there will be no others.
Come, learn a new song and sing it to me, for song
Is the means, in your beautiful voice, to alleviate sorrow.

(non enim posthac alia calebo
femina) condisce modos, amanda
voce quos reddas; minuentur atrae
  carmine curae.

Iam veris comites, quae mare temperant,
impellunt animae lintea Thraciae;
iam nec prata rigent nec fluvii strepunt
   hiberna nive turgidi.

Nidum ponit Ityn flebiliter gemens
infelix avis et Cecropiae domus
aeternum opprobrium, quod male barbaras
   regum est ulta libidines.

Dicunt in tenero gramine pinguium
custodes ovium carmina fistula
delectantque deum cui pecus et nigri
   colles Arcadiae placent.

Adduxere sitim tempora, Vergili;
sed pressum Calibus ducere Liberum
si gestis, iuvenum nobilium cliens,
   nardo vina merebere.

Nardi parvus onyx eliciet cadum,
qui nunc Sulpiciis accubat horreis,
spes donare novas largus amaraque
   curarum eluere efficax.

Ad quae si properas gaudia, cum tua
velox merce veni; non ego te meis
immunem meditor tinguere poculis,
   plena dives ut in domo.

Verum pone moras et studium lucri
nigrorumque memor, dum licet, ignium
misce stultitiam consiliis brevem;
   dulce est desipere in loco.

iv.12 / *To Vergilius*

Now the light tempering breezes, agents of Spring,
Are coming down from the fields of Thrace to fill
The sails of the little boats, so that at last

They begin to move about on the bay's calm waters.
The ice has gone from the fields; last week the roar
Of the rivers swollen with snow began to lessen.

And now the swallow, inheritrix of Procne,
Whose horrid revenge on the libidinous king
Brought down such shame, begins to build her nest,

Uttering tearful cries. On the tender grass
The shepherd sits, playing a song for the god
To whom the browsing as if listening flock

And the shadowy hills of Arcady give pleasure.
If you would share in the wine the season calls for,
A Calenian wine from the storehouse of Sulpicius,

Guaranteed efficacious in banishing care,
Then you must bring along a contribution,
A little onyx shell of fragrant spikenard.

Vergilius, don't forget to bring it, or
There'll be no wine for you. I'm not like one
Of those rich men who'd host you without caring

Whether or not you brought your share with you.
Leave off your serious business for a while,
Forget for a while ambition for place and money,

And, heedful of death's black fire, consent for a while
To mix a little pleasure in with your prudence.
It's right to be foolish when the time is right.

Audivere, Lyce, di mea vota, di
audivere, Lyce: fis anus et tamen
    vis formosa videri
        ludisque et bibis impudens

et cantu tremulo pota Cupidinem
lentum sollicitas. Ille virentis et
    doctae psallere Chiae
        pulchris excubat in genis.

Importunus enim transvolat aridas
quercus, et refugit te, quia luridi
    dentes te, quia rugae
        turpant et capitis nives.

Nec Coae referunt iam tibi purpurae
nec cari lapides tempora quae semel
    notis condita fastis
        inclusit volucris dies.

Quo fugit venus, heu, quove color? decens
quo motus? Quid habes illius, illius,
    quae spirabat amores,
        quae me surpuerat mihi,

felix post Cinaram notaque et artium
gratarum facies? Sed Cinarae brevis
    annos fata dederunt,
        servatura diu parem

cornicis vetulae temporibus Lycen,
possent ut iuvenes visere fervidi
    multo non sine risu
        dilapsam in cineres facem.

The gods have certainly given me what I asked for,
Lycia, Lycia, yes, they have certainly done so:
Lycia's getting old, and she wants to be
Still beautiful, and still she goes to parties,

And drinks too much and, a little teary, sings
A tremulous song meant for the ears of Cupid.
But Cupid's eyes are on Chia playing the lyre,
For Cupid scorns the old. So tell me, Lycia,

What is it you expect? Cupid scorns you.
He scorns your graying hair and yellowing teeth.
Old crow that watches from a dead oak tree
As wingèd Love flies by to another tree,

Neither your purple gowns of silk from Cos
Nor the costly jewels with which they are adorned
Can ever bring you back the things that time
Has locked away for good in its well-known box.

Where has your beauty gone, where has it gone,
Where is your fair complexion, where, alas,
The grace with which you walked? Lycia, you,
Whose breath was the very breath of love itself,

Who stole me from myself, oh, Lycia, you
Who exulted so when beautiful Cynara died,
Leaving your beauty unrivaled, where has it gone,
What is there left? When Cynara died young

The gods gave early death to her as a gift,
And, Lycia, they gave all your years to you
To give the young men something for them to laugh at,
Old crow, old torch burned out, fallen away to ashes.

Quae cura patrum quaeve Quiritium
plenis honorum muneribus tuas,
   Auguste, virtutes in aevum
     per titulos memoresque fastus

aeternet, o, qua sol habitabilis
illustrat oras, maxime principum,
   quem legis expertes Latinae
     Vindelici didicere nuper,

quid Marte posses? Milite nam tuo
Drusus Genaunos, implacidum genus,
   Breunosque velocis et arces
     Alpibus impositas tremendis

deiecit acer plus vice simplici;
maior Neronum mox grave proelium
   commisit immanisque Raetos
     auspiciis pepulit secundis,

spectandus in certamine Martio
devota morti pectora liberae
   quantis fatigaret ruinis,
     indomitas prope qualis undas

exercet Auster Pleïadum choro
scindente nubes, impiger hostium
   vexare turmas et frementem
     mittere equum medios per ignes.

Sic tauriformis volvitur Aufidus,
qui regna Dauni praefluit Apuli,
   cum saevit horrendamque cultis
     diluviem meditatur agris,

ut barbarorum Claudius agmina
ferrata vasto diruit impetu
   primosque et extremos metendo
     stravit humum sine clade victor,

Not all the bronze inscriptions that the Senate
And the Roman People have ordained could ever
Be adequate to tell the story of
Your deeds, Augustus, prince invincible,

Invincible wherever the sun shines down
On habitable countries; the Vindelici
Who boasted that they never had to know
The Roman law have now learned how to know it.

It was your army Drusus led when he
Brought down the obdurate Genauni, and
Brought down the swift Breuni and their strongholds
Built high among the peaks of tremendous Alps.

His elder brother then came into the battle
And under fortunate signs threw back the fierce
Rhaetians; a sight to see as he brought death
To those devoted to the death of men

Who cherish freedom. As when in the autumn sky
The Pleiades are seen through scudding clouds,
And the South Wind, roused, harries the furious waves,
So Claudius was eager to harass

The enemy host and rode his trumpeting horse
Into the midst of things. It was as when
The river Aufidus comes down like a bull
Into Apulia, raging and threatening flood—

Thus Claudius laid waste the enemy.
The ground was strewn with the armored corpses of
The fallen barbarians, struck down right and left,
Vanguard to rearguard, all without Roman loss.

The strategy of this great battle and
The heroes to carry it through were of Caesar's providing,
And so were the auspices of Fortune's favor.
For the day of this victory was the very same day,

te copias, te consilium et tuos
praebente divos. Nam tibi quo die
   portus Alexandrea supplex
      et vacuam patefecit aulam,

Fortuna lustro prospera tertio
belli secundos reddidit exitus,
   laudemque et optatum peractis
      imperiis decus arrogavit.

Te Cantaber non ante domabilis
Medusque et Indus, te profugus Scythes
   miratur, o tutela praesens
      Italiae dominaeque Romae.

Te, fontium qui celat origines,
Nilusque et Hister, te rapidus Tigris,
   te beluosus qui remotis
      obstrepit Oceanus Britannis,

te non paventis funera Galliae,
duraeque tellus audit Hiberiae,
   te caede gaudentes Sygambri
      compositis venerantur armis.

Three lustra before, when Alexandria
Surrendered and opened up her suppliant harbor,
And opened the doors of her empty palace to Caesar,
Bringing at last a happy end to the war.

The Cantabrian tribe no one had ever conquered,
The Medes, the Indians, the nomad Scythians marvel
At Caesar, protector of Rome and Italy.
The Nile whose source is a secret listens to you,

The Danube listens, the swift-flowing Tigris hears you,
The voice of Caesar's conquering power is heard
Echoing back from the cliffs of the British island
Over the monster-crowded ocean's roar.

The Gauls who thought they feared not death fear Caesar;
The land of the stubborn Iberians hears his voice;
The Sygambrians who vaunted their love of slaughter
Have now laid down their arms, in reverent silence.

Phoebus volentem proelia me loqui
victas et urbes increpuit lyra,
    ne parva Tyrrhenum per aequor
        vela darem. Tua, Caesar, aetas

fruges et agris rettulit uberes
et signa nostro restituit Iovi
    derepta Parthorum superbis
        postibus et vacuum duellis

Ianum Quirini clausit et ordinem
rectum evaganti frena licentiae
    iniecit emovitque culpas
        et veteres revocavit artis,

per quas Latinum nomen et Italae
crevere vires famaque et imperi
    porrecta maiestas ad ortus
        solis ab Hesperio cubili.

Custode rerum Caesare, non furor
civilis aut vis exiget otium,
    non ira, quae procudit enses
        et miseras inimicat urbes.

Non qui profundum Danuvium bibunt
edicta rumpent Iulia, non Getae,
    non Seres infidique Persae,
        non Tanaïn prope flumen orti.

Nosque et profestis lucibus et sacris
inter iocosi munera Liberi,
    cum prole matronisque nostris,
        rite deos prius apprecati,

I wanted to sing a heroic song about
Caesar's great victories in battle and
The conquering of cities, but Apollo
Struck a peremptory chord upon his lyre,
Forbidding me to do so, forbidding me
To launch my little boat on such an ocean.

Now in the time of Caesar the farms grow fat,
Burgeoning with plenty; Jupiter's temple
Is festive, hung once again with our Roman banners
Torn down from Parthian columns and brought home
Where they belong; the Janus gate is closed,
For there is peace. Caesar has closed the gate.

Caesar has put in order everything;
Caesar has set the bounds; has cast out vice;
And calls back home the ancient arts that our
Forefathers knew, by which the name of Rome
Is spread from where the sun comes up at dawn
Over to where the sun goes down at night.

While Caesar is in charge, be sure that peace
Will not be driven out by civil war
Within the city walls nor beaten down
By enemies from without; we shall be safe,
For Caesar guards us from the rage that is
The fire in which the swords of war are forged.

Neither the Vindelici, those who drink
The waters of the Danube near its source,
Nor the Parthians, the Getae, nor the Seres,
Nor the race whose native river is the Don,
Shall dare to break the laws he has laid down.
On working days or holy days we shall

Together with our children and our wives,
And with the gifts of Bacchus all around us,

virtute functos more patrum duces
Lydis remixto carmine tibiis
   Troiamque et Anchisen et almae
    progeniem Veneris canemus.

To Lydian music render up our prayers
To the generous gods, and, as our fathers did,
Sing hymns in praise of those who went before,
Venus's children, the offspring of Anchises.

CARMEN
SAECULARE

Phoebe silvarumque potens Diana,
lucidum caeli decus, o colendi
semper et culti, date quae precamur
     tempore sacro,

quo Sibyllini monuere versus
virgines lectas puerosque castos
dis quibus septem placuere colles
     dicere carmen.

Alme Sol, curru nitido diem qui
promis et celas aliusque et idem
nasceris, possis nihil urbe Roma
     visere maius!

Rite maturos aperire partus
lenis, Ilithyia, tuere matres,
sive tu Lucina probas vocari
     seu Genitalis.

Diva, producas subolem patrumque
prosperes decreta super iugandis
feminis prolisque novae feraci
     lege marita,

certus undenos deciens per annos
orbis ut cantus referatque ludos
ter die claro totiensque grata
     nocte frequentis.

Vosque veraces cecinisse, Parcae,
quod semel dictum est, stabilisque rerum
terminus servet, bona iam peractis
     iungite fata.

Carmen Saeculare

Phoebus Apollo, Diana, queen of the forests,
O deities the glories of the sky,
Most worthy to be worshiped, grant, we pray,
    Our prayers in the sacred season.

Now is the time the Sibylline Leaves ordain
That the chosen maidens and pure young men should sing
The poem written in honor of the gods
    Who favor the Seven Hills.

Beneficent sun who carries in the light
And bears it away again, born every day
Anew and yet the same, may sun never shine
    On any greater city.

Ilithyia, kind goddess, Genitalis,
Or Lucina, as you choose, whose kindness is
To bring to birth all things when they are ready,
    Watch over all mothers now.

Bring up our offspring tenderly, O goddess,
And foster well the Fathers' marriage laws
And bless new marriages that there may be
    New offspring to be blessed,

That joyful throngs, ten times eleven years
Come round again, may celebrate with songs
And festive games three days the sun shines on,
    Three moonlit joyful nights.

And may the Fates, having been true to us
In what they told, fulfill the prophecy
Until the end; may fortunate destiny
    Be joined to fortunate past.

Fertilis frugum pecorisque tellus
spicea donet Cererem corona;
nutriant fetus et aquae salubres
    et Iovis aurae.

Condito mitis placidusque telo
supplices audi pueros, Apollo;
siderum regina bicornis, audi,
    Luna, puellas.

Roma si vestrum est opus Iliaeque
litus Etruscum tenuere turmae,
iussa pars mutare Lares et urbem
    sospite cursu,

cui per ardentem sine fraude Troiam
castus Aeneas patriae superstes
liberum munivit iter, daturus
    plura relictis,

di, probos mores docili iuventae,
di, senectuti placidae quietem,
Romulae genti date remque prolemque
    et decus omne.

Quaeque vos bubus veneratur albis
clarus Anchisae Venerisque sanguis,
impetret, bellante prior, iacentem
    lenis in hostem.

Iam mari terraque manus potentis
Medus Albanasque timet securis,
iam Scythae responsa petunt superbi
    nuper et Indi.

Iam Fides et Pax et Honos Pudorque
priscus et neglecta redire Virtus
audet, apparetque beata pleno
    Copia cornu.

Fertile in crops and fertile in cattle too,
May Earth crown Ceres with a wheaten crown,
And may Jove's favoring rains and favoring breezes
    Ensure an abundant harvest.

Apollo, gentle and mild, put away your arrow,
Hearing the supplications of the youths;
And Luna, crescent queen of all the stars,
    Hear the young maidens.

Rome is your work, and those who came from Troy,
Bearing their household gods and seeking new homes,
Came to the Tuscan shore at your command,
    Watched over by you,

When pious Aeneas, he who survived the flames,
Made his dangerous journey across the seas,
Leading his people to freedom, and bringing with them
    More than they left behind.

O teach our young how to learn virtuous ways;
Give to our elders peaceable tranquil days;
And grant to all who descend from Romulus
    Prosperity and honor.

Grant what the heir of Anchises and of Venus
At the sacrifice of the milk-white oxen prays for:
That he may be victorious in conquest,
    Magnanimous to the conquered.

The Parthians fear our power on sea and land;
They fear the axes of our Alban warriors;
The Indians and Scythians once were scornful,
    And now they sue for peace.

Now Faith and Peace and ancient Modesty
And long-neglected Virtue and Honor dare
To return to be among us, and Plenty with
    Her cornucopia.

Augur et fulgente decorus arcu
Phoebus acceptusque novem Camenis,
qui salutari levat arte fessos
    corporis artus,

si Palatinas videt aequus aras,
remque Romanam Latiumque felix
alterum in lustrum meliusque semper
    prorogat aevum;

quaeque Aventinum tenet Algidumque,
quindecim Diana preces virorum
curat et votis puerorum amicas
    applicat auris.

Haec Iovem sentire deosque cunctos
spem bonam certamque domum reporto,
doctus et Phoebi chorus et Dianae
    dicere laudes.

Augur Apollo who carries the shining bow,
You whom the goddess Muses serve and adore,
You with your healing art, the medicine of
    Afflicted mind and body,

If the altars of the Palatine have pleased you,
May you preserve the happiness of Latium
And Rome's good fortune lustrum to lustrum ever
    Increasing ever after.

Diana whose haunt is cold Mount Algidus' side
And the temple on the Aventine, hear the prayers
Of the Fifteen Men who keep the Sibylline Books,
    And hear the prayers of the children.

Hopeful and certain that Jove and all the gods
Desire these things, now we return to our homes,
The choir chosen to sing the praises of
    Diana and Apollo.

Acknowledgments

Notes

Glossary

Acknowledgments

I have of course consulted a number of other translations and a number of commentaries. I am especially indebted for help with details of the translations to: C. E. Bennett, trans., *Horace: The Odes and Epodes*, The Loeb Classical Library (Cambridge, Mass.: Harvard University Press, 1964); James Michie, trans., *The Odes of Horace* (New York: Orion Press, 1963); R.G.M. Nisbet and Margaret Hubbard, eds., *A Commentary on Horace: Odes, Books I and II*, 2 vols. (Oxford: Oxford University Press, 1970, 1978); Paul Shorey and Gordon Laing, trans. and ed., *Horace: Odes and Epodes* (Pittsburgh: University of Pittsburgh Press, 1919); David Mulroy, trans., *Horace's Odes and Epodes* (Ann Arbor: University of Michigan Press, 1994); Rev. Philip Francis, trans., *Poetical Translations of the Works of Horace* (London, 1749). For help with the glossary I am indebted to J. E. Zimmerman, *Dictionary of Classical Mythology* (New York: Harper and Row, 1964).

A list of the many friends—critics and poets—who have helped and encouraged me in this project would be embarrassingly long. I am very grateful to them all, and to the editorial staff at Farrar, Straus and Giroux.

I owe special gratitude to those who have patiently answered my many questions about Horace's Latin: Wendell Clausen, Rodney Dennis, Katherine Geffcken, William L. Moran, Lawrence Rosenwald.

Most of all I thank Donald Carne-Ross and Anne Ferry.

I am grateful for the encouragement and financial support provided by an Award from the Ingram Merrill Foundation (1993), the Fellowship of the Academy of American Poets (1994), the Teasdale Prize for Poetry (1995), and a Fellowship from the John Simon Guggenheim Foundation (1996).

Notes

1. In a letter to this translator.
2. In his poem "A Thanksgiving," *Collected Poems*, ed. Edward Mendelson (New York: Random House, 1976), p. 671.
3. Oxford University Press, 1992, p. 451.

THE ODES
(Identifiable proper names are listed in the Glossary)

BOOK ONE

i.2 *"against the Tuscan shore"*: The high right bank of the Tiber, so that the waters were driven violently over the left bank.
    "that young man": Octavian, who became Augustus Caesar. He was Julius Caesar's great-nephew, seen here as avenger of Julius Caesar's assassination.

i.3 The last of Hercules' Twelve Labors required him to go down to the Underworld and dognap Cerberus, the monstrous guard dog of Hades.

i.4 *Lycidas*: A conventional name. It occurs in one of Virgil's eclogues.

i.5 *Pyrrha*: R.G.M. Nisbet and Margaret Hubbard, *A Commentary on Horace: Odes, Book I* (Oxford: Oxford University Press, 1970), suggest that the name itself refers to her blondness.
    I stole *"Hapless"* from Milton's great translation of this ode.
    "The votive tablet on the temple wall": ". . . rescued sailors sometimes dedicated their clothes *ex voto* to the gods" (Nisbet and Hubbard, *A Commentary on Horace*, note on this poem). See *The Greek Anthology*, with all its "dedicatory epigrams," in which representatives of various occupations—farmers, soldiers, artisans, musicians—deposit the tools of their trade in the temples of the appropriate gods. See, for example, epigram 70: "O King of the sea and lord of the land, I, Crantas, dedicate to thee this my ship, no longer immersed in the sea—my ship, bird blown by the wandering winds, in which I, poor wretch, often thought I was being driven to Hades. Now, having renounced them all, fear, hope, sea, storms, I plant my steps confidently on dry land"; from *The Greek Anthology*, W. R. Paton, trans., The Loeb Classical Library, 5 vols. (Cambridge, Mass.: Harvard University Press, 1980), vol. I, p. 337.
    "in tribute to the god": Nisbet and Hubbard refer to suggestions by some scholars that it should be Venus, the goddess of love, to whom the votive tablet is dedicated. See iii.26 and the note to that poem.

i.6 *"in battle against two gods"*: Diomedes wounded both Venus and Mars in battle.

i.8 *Lydia* and *Sybaris* are conventional names. His name is suggestive.
    Achilles' mother got him to hide out, dressed as a woman, on the island of Skyros.

i.9 The name *Thaliarchus* has festive Greek associations.
    I have rendered the final quatrain very freely.

i.10 *"You stole away / Priam from Troy"*: See the *Iliad*, XXIV, 334ff.

i.11 *Leuconoë*: A conventional name.
   "Ouija board" is a modern substitution for the less familiar "Babylonian num-
   bers," which a literal translation of *Babylonios . . . numeros* would have pro-
   duced.

i.12 *"as his mother taught him"*: Orpheus's mother was the Muse Calliope. His father
   was Apollo.
   "the virgin goddess who / Chastises all the beasts": Diana the huntress.
   "the twin sons of Leda": Castor and Pollux.

i.13 *Lydia, Telephus*: Conventional names.

i.14 The poem is based on a fragment of a poem by Alcaeus. Petrarch adapted this
   political ode by Horace to the purposes of a love poem, *"Passa la nave . . ."*
   (*Rime* 189), of which Sir Thomas Wyatt made a famous translation, "My galley
   chargèd with forgetfulness."
   "Your onboard gods": Images of the household gods carried on shipboard for
   good luck.

i.15 *"becoming a sea bird"*: I have taken advantage of Horace's figure of speech *mala
   . . . avi* to turn Nereus literally into a bird of prophetic ill-omen.
   "Laertes' son": Ulysses.
   "Tydeus' terrible son": Diomedes.

i.16 *Helena*: Not Helen of Troy but some real or fictitious young woman whom
   Horace had sent real or fictitious offensive poems to.

i.17 *Tyndaris*: A conventional name. Principal stress on the first syllable.
   Cyrus: A conventional name.

i.18 *Varus*: The identity of this addressee is not at all certain. Some editors think
   he is the Quintilius of i.24. It is evident from the poem that he is a prosperous
   man who owns vineyards at Tibur.
   This poem is more free as a translation than some of the others. Obviously
   there is no warrant in the Latin for the bar or the barfly, and the last two lines
   are almost entirely my invention.

i.19 *Glycera*: A conventional name, perhaps for a courtesan. Etymologically the
   name suggests slipperiness. Principal stress on the first syllable.

i.20 For Maecenas's illness and the public jubilation at his recovery, see also ii.17.
   The scene of jubilation was the Theater of Pompey.

i.21 *Choristers*: Ritual choruses of boys and young maidens. See also iv.6 and the
   Carmen Saeculare.
   "his brother": Hermes (Mercury).
   Apollo, especially, is protector of Rome.

i.22 *Lalage*: A conventional name. Three syllables, principal stress on the first.

i.23 *Chloë*: A conventional name.

i.24 See note to i.18.
   "The god whose horrid wand": Mercury.

i.25 *Lydia*: A conventional name.

i.26 This poem is addressed to a member of the distinguished Lamia family. See
   also i.36 and iii.17.

i.27 *Megylla*: A conventional name.

i.28 There has been scholarly disagreement about whether this is one poem or two
   (ll. 1–20 of the Latin; 21–end) and about how to assign the speaker's or speak-
   ers' voice or voices. Some recent translations read the poem as spoken by one
   speaker throughout, the ghost of an unburied drowned sailor addressing the

dead Archytas and then imploring (with threats) a passerby to bury his body. I have chosen to read it as a poem in two parts, with two speakers: the first the voice of a traveler who has come upon the grave of Archytas the Pythagorean philosopher, the second the voice of the unburied drowned sailor addressing that same sophisticated traveler. To my ear the voice in the first part of the poem, learned, worldly, sardonic, is very different from the voice in the second part, much simpler, beggarly, primitive, elemental, magical.

"*The father of Pelops*": Tantalus.

i.29   *Iccius*: This bookworm has not been certainly identified.

Chinese: The Seres.

i.30   *Glycera*: A conventional name, perhaps for a courtesan. Principal stress on the first syllable.

"*the amorous boy*": Cupid.

i.31   "*As on his day . . .*": Apollo's temple on the Palatine was dedicated October 9, 28 B.C.E.

i.32   There has been disagreement, based on manuscript discrepancies, about whether the first phrase in the Latin is *Poscimus* or *Poscimur*. Some translators therefore read the opening phrase as "We are (or I am) asked for a song." I've chosen the other reading (using Nisbet and Hubbard's commentary as my excuse) because it seems more appropriate to the prayer which is the poem.

"*The child who clings to her*": Cupid.

i.33   Addressed to the poet Tibullus.

All the men's and women's names (except for Albius) are conventional. All the trisyllabic names (which include Myrtale) are principally stressed on the first syllable.

i.35   "*Then Hope and Faith . . . make their departure too*": There has been some disagreement among scholars about the lines translated this way. Some have argued that Hope and Faith are to be understood as faithfully remaining when the household is in trouble. When scholars disagree, the translator has an opportunity to choose between them.

"*a spike, and a wedge,*" etc.: Instruments traditionally associated with Fortuna and therefore carried by her attendant Necessitas.

i.36   Numida hasn't been identified, but Lamia refers to some member of the distinguished Lamia family. See also Odes i.26 and iii.17.

Bassus and Damalis: Conventional names. Damalis should be pronounced with the main stress on the first syllable.

i.37   The occasion of the poem is news of the final defeat and the deaths of Antony and Cleopatra (30 B.C.E.).

BOOK TWO

ii.1   Cato the Younger.

ii.3   *the Sisters*: The Parcae, the three Fates.

"*that dark boat*": The boat of Charon, the oarsman of the river Styx.

ii.4   *Xanthias* has not been identified.

Atrides: Agamemnon. The captive was the Trojan princess Cassandra.

Phyllis: A conventional name.

ii.5   *Lalage, Pholoë, Chloris, Gyges*: Conventional names. This Gyges is supposed to be from Cnidos, a Greek town in Asia Minor.

ii.6   *Septimius*: A friend of Horace's, not identified.
        "that wild mountainous land": Cantabria, a region of northern Spain.
ii.7   Horace, and this Pompey, had been in the army of Brutus and Cassius, fighting
        against Octavian (Augustus). Philippi is the disastrous battle that ended the
        cause of Brutus and Cassius, who committed suicide. Horace's property was
        confiscated but he was allowed to go to Rome, where he later came into favor
        with Augustus. This real or fictitious Pompey was evidently forgiven later and
        had been allowed to return to Italy only a short time before the occasion, real
        or fictitious, of the poem.
ii.8   *Barina*: A conventional name.
ii.9   *Mystes*: Perhaps a slave boy. Two syllables.
ii.11   *Lyde*: One of the conventional names for the women in these poems. Lyde
        appears in several, sometimes perhaps as Horace's housekeeper. Two sylla-
        bles.
ii.12   I have translated the last few lines more freely than usual.
ii.13   *Prometheus* should be heard as a four-syllable word in this rendering.
ii.14   *"Giants he holds in thrall"*: Tityos and Geryon.
        "Danaus' wicked daughters": see iii.11.
ii.15   *Cato the Censor*: "later ages saw in him an exemplar of old Roman virtue";
        R.G.M. Nisbet and Margaret Hubbard, *A Commentary on Horace: Odes, Book II*,
        (Oxford: Oxford University Press, 1978), note on this poem.
ii.16   *"for rendering Grecian verses"*: For bringing into Latin poetry the verse-practices,
        metrical and otherwise, he learned from Greek poets like Alcaeus and Sappho.
        See iii.30.
ii.18   *"Tantalus' son"*: Pelops, founder of the house of Atreus. Killed by his father.
ii.19   Pentheus is pronounced as a trisyllabic word in this rendering; principal stress
        on the first syllable.
        "wearing his golden horns": *aureo / cornu decorum* has been variously interpreted,
        for example, as Bacchus carrying a horn.
ii.20   Interesting to compare this poem to iii.30, the last poem in Book Three.

BOOK THREE

iii.1   *"the Kid"*: Haedus, a constellation whose rising, in the autumn, was a cause
        of storms.
        "Dog Star heat": The star Sirius rises at the hottest time of summer.
iii.2   *"The secret rites and mysteries of Ceres"*: The Eleusinian Mysteries of the worship
        of Demeter (the Greek Ceres). Death was the punishment for revealing them.
iii.3   *"the foreign woman"*: Helen.
        "the corrupted judge": Paris, who offended Juno by choosing Venus over Juno
        (and Minerva) in the famous beauty contest between them.
        "When Priam's royal father broke his promise": Laomedon, king of Troy, refused
        to recompense Apollo and Neptune, who had been sent by Jupiter to help
        build the walls of Troy. As a result, Laomedon and all his sons except Priam
        were killed.
        ". . . the infamous guest in her husband's house": Paris, the guest in Menelaus's
        house.
        "so long may the Capitol shine": The temple on the Capitoline hill in Rome.
        "Let the Romans go to the limits of the world, / Not for the sake of plunder but for

the sake / Of extending Roman knowledge everywhere": I found *visere gestiens* hard to bring over into English without (wrongly) giving the impression that Juno was giving the Romans permission to conquer the world just to satisfy their curiosity. I notice that Philip Francis, in his eighteenth-century translation, apparently ran into the same problem and interpreted the lines in a similar way.

iii.4 *"You know the story of how the Titans . . ."*: In the following lines Horace conflates the stories of the Titans' wars against the Olympians and the later war of the Giants against the Olympians.

"the brothers determined to pile up mountains": Otus and Ephialtes, two Giants.

"he who sought / To take Proserpina": Pirithous, king of the Lapiths.

iii.5 Horace's instance of the behavior of Crassus's soldiers dates from two centuries later than what Regulus already saw, already understood, in 251 B.C.E.

iii.7 *Asteria, Gyges, Chloë, Enipeus*: Conventional names.

"the Wild Goat / Constellation": Haedus, its rising thought to cause storms.

"the Campus": The Campus Martius, where athletes exercised.

iii.8 The first of March was the Matronalia, in honor of marriage.

iii.9 *Chloë, Calais, Ornytus, Lydia*: Conventional names.

iii.10 I have substituted "Lycia" for Horace's "Lyce," because the pronunciation of "Lyce" isn't immediately clear in English.

"Lest the rope run backward as the wheel does too": Borrowed in part from *Horace: The Odes and Epodes*, trans. C. E. Bennett, The Loeb Classical Library (Cambridge, Mass.: Harvard University Press, 1964).

iii.11 *Lyde*: A conventional name, pronounced as two syllables.

Danaus, the legendary king of Apulia, was conquered by his enemy Aegyptus, king of the Egyptians, who demanded that Danaus's fifty daughters marry Aegyptus's sons. They did so but were ordered by their father to murder their husbands during their wedding night. All but one of them did so. In the version of the legend that Horace uses, the murderous daughters were punished by being condemned forever to pour water into a bottomless urn.

iii.12 *Neobule, Hebrus*: Conventional names.

iii.13 *Bandusian fountain*: A spring and little waterfall on Horace's Sabine estate.

iii.14 *"the sister"*: Augustus's sister Octavia.

Neaera: A conventional name.

iii.15 *Ibycus, Pholoë, Nothus*: Conventional names.

iii.16 *"the Argive prophet"*: Eriphyle, the wife of Amphiaraus, accepted the offer of a gold necklace as a reward for persuading her husband to join the disastrous war against Thebes. Though Amphiaraus knew how it would end, he went, and was killed. Eriphyle was killed by Alcmaeon, their son.

"Maecenas, glory of simple knighthood": Maecenas, in spite of his wealth and high office, kept the rank of *eques*, knight. (On the other hand, Maecenas was known to like ostentatious display of his wealth.)

"Laestrygonian wine": A fine wine from Formiae.

iii.18 *"We celebrate your day"*: December 5.

iii.19 *Codrus*, the legendary last Attic king, deliberately got himself killed to save his country.

Telephus, Lycus, Glycera: Conventional names.

Murena: Identification uncertain. Perhaps this is Licinius, ii.10. See Glossary.

cyathi: A cyathus was a ladle for pouring wine into goblets.

iii.20 *Pyrrhus, Nearchus*: Conventional names.

iii.23 *Phidyle*: A conventional rural name, etymologically derived from the Greek for "thrift."

iii.24 *trochus Graecus*: A sissy game played by trundling rattling hoops.

iii.26 See last note to i.5. It may be significant that this dedicatory epigram occurs so near the end of the third book of the odes, since Books One through Three were published as a complete work. Horace is in a sense laying down, or pretending to lay down, the tools of his amatory trade as a lover and as a writer. See, for example, in *The Greek Anthology*, epigram 80: "I am the nine books of Agathias Daphniad, and he who composed me dedicates me to thee, Aphrodite. For I am not so dear to the Muses as to Love, since I treat of the mysteries of so many loves. In return for his pains he begs thee to grant him either not to love or to love one who soon consents"; from *The Greek Anthology*, trans. W. R. Paton, The Loeb Classical Library, 5 vols. (Cambridge, Mass.: Harvard University Press, 1980), vol. I, p. 343.

I borrow *"uplifted lash"* directly from C. E. Bennett, trans., *Horace: The Odes and Epodes*, The Loeb Classical Library (Cambridge, Mass.: Harvard University Press, 1964), and *"flick"* directly from James Michie, trans., *The Odes of Horace* (New York: Orion Press, 1963).

iii.27 *Galatea*: A conventional name.

iii.28 *Lyde*: A conventional name. Perhaps his housekeeper. Two syllables.

iii.29 *Tuscan*: Etruscan.

"the lesser Dog Star": Procyon. Leo, the Dog Stars, Cepheus, Andromeda are midsummer stars and constellations associated with extreme heat.

Seres, Bactrians, Scythians: All of these people are very remote; not much to worry about.

iii.30 Books One through Three were originally published together, so this was the last poem in that collection.

"the death goddess": Libitina, goddess of corpses, registrar of the dead.

Pontiff: A high priest.

Vestal: Priestess of the goddess Vesta.

"Aeolian measures": Horace adapted to Latin the meters (and many other characteristics) of the poems of the Aeolian poets Sappho and Alcaeus. In this connection see especially ii.13, ii.16, and i.32.

"Delphic laurel": There was a shrine to Apollo, god of poetry, on Mount Parnassus at Delphi.

BOOK FOUR

iv.1 *Cynara*: A conventional name.

Ligurinus: A conventional name. It could mean that he came from Liguria, the Piedmont region. But there is a verb, *ligurire*, "to lust after."

iv.4 *"Who sprang from the ground where the dragon's teeth were sown"*: They were sown by Jason, leader of the Argonauts. The crop was a troop of soldiers.

iv.6 Mainly addressed to Apollo, as a kind of hymn. The last fourteen lines are addressed to the boys and girls who are being rehearsed to sing the hymn. The poem is closely associated with the Carmen Saeculare.

"ten times eleven years": The canonical period separating celebrations of the Saecular Games.

iv.7 *Torquatus*: A member of a distinguished Roman family.

iv.9 *"someone's adulterous elegant hairdo"*: Paris's. This Trojan prince ran off with Helen, Menelaus's wife, and thus occasioned the Trojan War.

iv.10 *Ligurinus*: Not identified otherwise. See also iv.1 and note.

iv.11 *Phyllis* and *Telephus*: Conventional names.

iv.12 There is a disagreement among scholars about whether or not the person addressed in this poem is the poet Virgil. Because there is disagreement I have felt free to choose and have elected to treat it as if the Vergilius of this poem was not the poet but a young man of the world, ambitious in a quite different way. The line *Verum pone moras et studium lucri* seems hard to apply to Virgil the poet.

iv.13 *Chia, Cynara*: Conventional names. In Horace the woman who is addressed (and talked about) is called Lyce, also a conventional name. I have called her Lycia, which is easier to pronounce in English. See also iii.10, where I've made the same substitution.

iv.14 *"His elder brother"*: Claudius, who became the emperor Tiberius.
"Three lustra before, when Alexandria / Surrendered and opened up her suppliant harbor": This refers to the fall of Cleopatra and the end of Augustus's war against Mark Antony, 30 B.C.E. A lustrum is a period of five years.

iv.15 *"the Janus gate is closed"*: As the lines indicate, the gates of the Janus Temple were closed when there was peace, open when there was war, symbolizing the ability of the Romans to go out to defend themselves. The gate had been closed only twice before the reign of Augustus.

CARMEN SAECULARE

Sibylline Books: Greek hexameter verses, supposedly oracular, deposited in the temple of Apollo on the Palatine. The *quindecim viri*, the Fifteen Men, were its keepers, and it was their convenient interpretation of the oracles which permitted Augustus to stage his Saecular festivities on the date he wanted. Horace was commissioned by Augustus to write the Saecular Hymn, which was performed by a chorus of boys and girls on this occasion.

Ilythia, Lucina: Birth goddesses, here intended to be identified with Diana, who is also, among other things, a birth goddess.

Genitalis: A name parallel in meaning and function to Ilythia and Lucina, but apparently invented by Horace for this purpose.

"ten times eleven years": The Saecular festivities were supposed to occur at some such interval.

Luna: The moon, here another name for Diana, goddess of the moon.

"the heir of Anchises and of Venus": Augustus was a descendant of Aeneas, who was the son of the goddess Venus and the Trojan prince Anchises.

Glossary

*(This does not include the fictional or conventional names
Horace uses in a number of the poems.)*

A C H A E A N : Achaia, a region of Greece. The adjective often refers to the Greeks or Grecian things in general.

A C H A E M E N E S : Mythical founder of the rich Persian dynasty.

A C H E R O N : One of the five rivers of Hades.

A C H E R O N T I A , B A N T I A , F O R E N T U M : Towns in Apulia near Horace's birthplace, Venusia.

A C H I L L E S : The greatest of the warriors against Troy; slayer of Hector.

A C R O C E R A U N I A : A mountainous headland in what is now Albania; the "Thunder Mountain."

A E A C U S : One of the judges in the Underworld. Son of Zeus and Aegina. Three syllables, principal stress on the first.

A E N E A S : A son of Venus (Aphrodite) and of the Trojan prince Anchises. He survived the Trojan War and took his father and a remnant of the Trojans to Italy, where they established the civilization that became Rome.

A E O L I A N : Associated with the poets Alcaeus and Sappho, both of them from the island of Lesbos, which was inhabited by Aeolians, a Grecian people immigrating to the island from Asia Minor; also associated with Aeolus, the god of the winds, and his mythical floating island Aeolia.

A E T N A : A great volcano in Sicily.

A G A M E M N O N : Son of Atreus; brother of Menelaus. He was the king of the Myceneans and of Argos; the grand chieftain of the Greeks against the Trojans.

A G R I P P A : Marcus Vipsanius Agrippa was Augustus's chief military leader, whether by land or sea. He married Augustus's daughter Julia.

A G Y I E U S : Apollo's name as protector of streets.

A J A X : One of the greatest warriors against the Trojans.

A L B A N : A region of hills near Rome. Soldiers from this region were supposed to be especially good at their work; a wine-producing region.

A L B A N U S , M O U N T : A mountain near Rome.

A L B I U S T I B U L L U S : The poet Tibullus, Horace's friend.

A L B U N E A : A grotto in the region of Horace's Sabine house.

A L C A E U S : Poet of the seventh century B.C.E., from the island of Lesbos. He fought against tyrants. Horace greatly admired his poems and adapted his meters to Latin.

A L E X A N D R I A : Cleopatra's capital, in Egypt.

A L G I D U S , M O U N T : A mountain near Rome. Principal stress on the first syllable.

A M A Z O N I A N : Pertaining to the Amazons, female warriors who lived in Asia Minor.

A M O R I N I : The little cupid attendants of Venus.

A M P H I O N : Son of Jove and a mortal, Antiope. Amphion was a musician and the builder of the walls of Thebes.

A N A C R E O N : A sixth-century B.C.E. writer of convivial and erotic songs.

A N C H I S E S : Father of Aeneas.

A N C U S M A R T I U S : An early king of Rome.

A N I O : Tibur's river, a tributary of the Tiber.

A N T I L O C H U S : Son of Nestor killed in the Trojan War. Principal stress on the second syllable.

A N T I O C H U S : King of Syria, second century B.C.E., defeated by the Romans. Principal stress on the second syllable.

A N T I U M : A seaside town south of Rome; the modern name is Anzio.

A P O L L O : Son of Zeus and Latona; brother of Diana. Born on the island of Delos. Sun god, god of the arts, god of healing, god protector of cities.

A P U L I A : A southeastern region of Italy where Horace was born.

A R C A D I A (A R C A D Y) : A region of the central Peloponnesus, treated in some literature as an idyllic landscape, where the nature god Pan dwells.

A R C H Y T A S : A philosopher and mathematician of the fourth century B.C.E. He came from Tarentum in Apulia, Horace's native region. Principal stress on the second syllable.

A R C T U R U S : A constellation whose setting, in the autumn, was thought to be a cause of storms.

A R G O S : A city in the Peloponnesus famous for its horses.

A R I A D N E : After she helped Theseus escape from the labyrinth of the Minotaur they were married, but Theseus left her on Naxos, Bacchus's island. She became Bacchus's wife.

A T H E N A : Goddess of wisdom. Her Roman name is Minerva.

A T L A S : Atlas (the Atlas Mountains) supports the world on his shoulders. Atlas was a Titan, a son of Zeus, and the father of Maia.

A T R E U S : The father of Agamemnon and Menelaus and brother of Thyestes, whom he deceived into eating his own children.

A T R I D E S : Agamemnon.

A U F I D U S : An Apulian river.

A U G U S T U S : Octavian Caesar, the first of the Roman emperors.

A U L O N : Near Tarentum, praised by Horace for its wines.

A V E N T I N E : One of the Seven Hills of Rome, where there was a temple of Diana.

B A C C H A N T E : A female follower of Bacchus; a Maenad.

B A C C H U S : Roman name for Dionysus. God of wine, festivity, inspiration, and, in some contexts, moderation.

B A C T R I A N S : A people dwelling in what is now Afghanistan.

B A I A E : A seaside town on the Bay of Naples.

B E L L E R O P H O N : He killed the Chimera. He tried to ride to heaven on his horse Pegasus, and died as a result.

B E R E C Y N T H I A N : Berecyntus was a mountain in Thrace associated with the revels of Cybele. Berecynthian horns were used in these rites and in Dionysian (Bacchic) rites as well.

B I B U L U S : Consul in 59 B.C.E., with Julius Caesar.

B I T H Y N I A : A forested region on the Black Sea inhabited by a warlike people, famous also as shipbuilders.

B L E S S E D I S L E : Where the favored go after death; the Elysian Fields.

B O S P O R U S : The straits between the Black Sea and the Sea of Marmara, separating Europe from Asia.

B R E U N I : A tribe dwelling in what are now the Tyrolean Alps.

334

B R I S E I S : The young woman who was the bone of contention between Achilles and Agamemnon, causing Achilles to withdraw from the war. Principal stress on the second syllable.

B R U T U S : Marcus Brutus. Leader of the assassins of Julius Caesar. Defeated at Philippi, 42 B.C.E., by Octavian (Augustus) and Mark Antony.

B Y T H I N I A : Timber for ships often came from this region in Asia Minor.

C Á D I Z : The modern name for Gades.

C A E C U B A N : A fine wine from Latium.

C A L A B R I A : In modern times the name refers to the southwestern region of Italy, the toe of the boot; in ancient times it referred to the southeastern region, the heel of the boot.

C A L E N I A N : A fine wine from Cales, in the Campania.

C A L L I O P E : Daughter of Zeus and Mnemosyne. Muse of heroic poetry. Mother of Orpheus.

C A M I L L U S : M. Furius Camillus, hero in the Gallic Wars, c. 300 B.C.E.

C A M P A N I A : A region east of Rome.

C A M P U S   M A R T I U S : A part of Rome where athletes exercised. The Theater of Pompey was located there.

C A N T A B R I A N S : A tribe dwelling in northern Spain.

C A P I T O L : The Capitolium, the temple of Jupiter on the Capitoline.

C A P I T O L I N E : One of the Seven Hills of Rome.

C A R T H A G E : The principal city of the Phoenicians, enemies and rivals of Rome.

C A S T A L I A N : A sacred spring on the side of Mount Parnassus.

C A S T O R   A N D   P O L L U X : Castor the horseman and Pollux the boxer, sons of Leda, whom Zeus seduced, taking the form of a swan. Their sisters were Helen and Clytemnestra. After their death they became the Gemini. As stars they were thought to calm the waters.

C A T I L L U S ,   M O U N T : A mountain near Tibur (Tivoli).

C A T O : Cato the Censor, second century B.C.E., who exemplified the austere values of the old Republic.
Cato the Younger fought against Julius Caesar, and committed suicide when he was defeated.

C E N S O R I N U S : Gaius Marcius Censorinus, who became consul in 8 B.C.E.

C E N T A U R S   A N D   L A P I T H S : The Lapiths were Thessalians, all of them killed in the drunken battle with the Centaurs, beings who were half-horse, half-man.

C E R B E R U S : The three-headed watchdog of the Underworld.

C E R E S : Goddess of agriculture.

C H A R Y B D I S : Daughter of Poseidon and Gaea, sea and earth, who became a monstrous whirlpool off the coast of Italy.

C H I M E R A : A monster with a goat body, lion head, and serpent tail, and a breath of fire. Killed by Bellerophon. Stress on the second syllable.

C I R C E : The sorceress who turned Ulysses' men into swine and who bewitched and seduced Ulysses.

C L A U D I A N   H O U S E : Tiberius Claudius Nero's widow, Livia, married Augustus, who adopted her sons, Drusus and Tiberius.

C L A U D I U S   (T I B E R I U S) : Augustus's stepson, son of Augustus's wife Livia and her first husband, Tiberius Claudius Nero. He became the emperor Tiberius.

CLEOPATRA: The last Ptolemaic ruler; lover of Julius Caesar and then of Mark Antony. Defeated at Actium, 31 B.C.E. Antony and Cleopatra committed suicide a year later, and Octavian's (Augustus's) supremacy was completely assured.

CLIO: The Muse of history.

CNIDOS: A Greek city in Asia Minor with a famous statue of Aphrodite by Praxiteles.

COCYTOS: One of the five rivers of Hades.

CODRUS: The ancient last king of Athens.

COLCHIANS: A people living near the Black Sea.

CONCANIANS: A Spanish tribe.

CORINTH: A Grecian city that looks over both the Ionian and the Aegean Seas.

CORVINUS: M. Valerius Messalla Corvinus. Commanded troops against Octavian (Augustus) and Mark Antony at Philippi. Later a general under Antony. Still later a commander of Octavian's fleet when Antony was defeated at Actium. Patron of the poet Tibullus.

CORYBANTIC: The Corybantes were priests of Cybele.

COS: An island in the Aegean.

COTISO: A Dacian commander defeated by the Romans in 30 B.C.E.

CRASSUS: A Roman general defeated by the Parthians in 53 B.C.E.

CRETE: A large island in the Mediterranean.

CROESUS: A Lydian king, the richest man in the world.

CURIUS: M. Curius Dentatus. He fought gloriously in the Pyrrhic War (281–275 B.C.E.).

CYCLADES: A chain of islands in the Aegean.

CYPRUS: A large island in the Mediterranean associated with Venus.

CYRUS: Founder of the Persian empire.

DACIANS: A warlike people in Transylvania.

DAEDALUS: The artificer who made, among other things, wings to fly with. He flew and so did his son Icarus, whose wing-fastenings melted when he flew too near the sun, with a calamitous result.

DALMATIA: A region on the eastern coast of the Adriatic.

DAMOCLES: Damocles envied the rich tyrant of Syracuse, who taught Damocles a lesson by showing how a sword perpetually hovered over his head.

DANAË: Ravished by Zeus in the form of a shower of gold.

DANAUS: Mythical king of Apulia.

DEIPHOBUS: A great Trojan warrior; Hector's brother.

DELIAN: Having to do with Delos, Apollo's birthplace, and Diana's.

DELLIUS: Quintus Dellius, "circus rider of the civil wars," served Crassus, then Antony, then Augustus. A rich man, he enjoyed his riches.

DELOS: The island on which Apollo and Diana were born.

DELPHI: The site of an Apollonian oracle on Mount Parnassus.

DIANA: Goddess of the moon, of chastity, of the hunt, of childbirth. Apollo's sister.

DINDYMENE: A name for the fertility goddess Cybele. Four syllables, stressed on the first and third.

DIOMEDES: One of the greatest heroes of the Trojan war. Son of Tydeus, king of Tiryns.

DIRCE: The fountain of Dirce, near Thebes, Pindar's birthplace.

D O N : The modern name of the river Tanais.

D R U S U S : Augustus's stepson, son of Augustus's wife Livia and her first husband, Tiberius Claudius Nero.

E B R O : A river in Spain.

E N C E L A D U S : Giant who warred against the Olympian gods.

E P H E S U S : A Grecian city in Asia Minor.

E R Y M A N T H U S : A mountain in Arcadia, in the Peloponnesus.

E U P H O R B U S : A Trojan warrior killed by Menelaus.

E U P H R A T E S : A river in Mesopotamia.

E U R O P A : Zeus took the form of a bull and carried her off to Cyprus.

E U R U S : The East Wind.

E U T E R P E : The Muse of flute playing.

F A B R I C I U S : He fought gloriously in the Pyrrhic War (281–275 B.C.E.).

F A L E R N I A N : A choice Roman wine.

F A L E R N U M : A town in the Campania, near Rome, where the Falernian wine comes from.

F A T E S : Atropos, Clotho, Lachesis. In Latin, the Fatae or the Parcae. They determine when you will die.

F A U N U S : A god of the country, of agriculture, and of rural festivity, and, Horace says in ii.17, a "protector of poets"; the Roman god closest to Pan in attributes.

F I F T E E N   M E N : Designated keepers and interpreters of the oracular sayings in the Sibylline Books.

F O R M I A N : A fine wine from Formiae, in Latium.

F U R I E S : Alecto, Megaera, Tisiphone; the Avengers.

F U S C U S : Aristius Fuscus, a poet and grammarian; Horace's friend.

G A L E A S U S : A river near Tibur (Tivoli).

G A L L I C : Of Gaul.

G A N Y M E D E : A Trojan youth carried off by Zeus to be his cupbearer in heaven.

G A R G A N O ,   M O U N T : A promontory in northern Apulia.

G A T E S   O F   H E R C U L E S : The Strait of Gibraltar.

G A U L S : A people living in what is now France, Belgium, and part of western Germany.

G E L O N I A N S   (G E L O N I) : A warlike Scythian tribe.

G E N A U N I : A tribe dwelling in what are now the Tyrolean Alps.

G E R Y O N : A three-headed three-bodied monster.

G E T A E : A warlike people dwelling around the lower Danube.

G I A N T S : The children of Uranus and Gaea, they warred against the Olympians and were defeated by the gods, with the help of Hercules.

G R A C E S : Aglaia, Euphrosyne, Thalia, personifications of beneficent grace and gracefulness, in Venus's retinue.

G R O S P H U S : Pompeius Grosphus, a very rich Sicilian landowner.

G Y A S : A hundred-handed monster.

H A D E S : The Underworld; also, the god of the Underworld.

H A E D U S : A constellation associated with stormy weather.

H A E M U S ,   M O U N T : A mountain in Thrace associated with Orpheus.

H A N N I B A L : The Carthaginian general finally defeated by the Romans in 202 B.C.E.

H A S D R U B A L : The leader of the Carthaginians in the second Punic War, in the third century B.C.E.

HEBRUS: A river in Thrace.

HECTOR: Troy's most formidable defender.

HELEN: Menelaus's wife. Her seduction by Paris caused the Trojan War.

HELICON: A mountain in Greece where the Hippocrene fountain, sacred to the Muses, flowed.

HERCULES: Son of Zeus and Alcmena. Performed the Twelve Labors. Sometimes worshiped as a god, and in Horace's account he indeed became a god.

HESPERIA: The West, western Europe.

HIMERA: A town on the north coast of Sicily.

HIPPOLYTA: This Hippolyta (not the Queen of the Amazons) accused the father of Achilles, Peleus, who had refused her, of assaulting her sexually.

HIPPOLYTUS: Phaedra, Theseus's wife, tried to seduce Hippolytus, Theseus's son. He refused her and she made false accusations about him to Theseus. Hippolytus died trying to escape the vengeance of his father.

HYADES: A constellation associated with rain and storms.

HYDASPES: A river in the Indian subcontinent.

HYDRA: A nine-headed serpent killed by Hercules.

HYMETTUS: A mountain in Greece famous for its honey.

HYPERBOREANS: A mythical people inhabiting the cold far North.

IBERIANS: Inhabitants of the Spanish Peninsula.

ICARUS: His father made wings of wax and feathers for Icarus and himself, so that they could escape from Crete. Icarus flew too high and the sun melted the wax, so he fell into what came to be called the Icarian Sea. Principal stress on the first syllable.

IDA: A mountain which was the source of many rivers.

IDOMENEUS: A king of Crete, valiant in the Trojan War.

ILIA: A Vestal Virgin who was seduced by Mars and gave birth to Romulus and Remus. She was then drowned in the river Tiber and became the river's wife.

ILITHYIA: Goddess of childbirth. Also Lucina, Genitalis, names associated with deities of childbirth, used by Horace as synonyms for Diana.

ILIUM: Troy.

INACHUS: The earliest king of Argos.

IULLUS ANTONIUS: The son of Mark Antony by his first wife, Fulvia. Raised in the house of Octavia, Antony's second wife, the sister of Augustus. He had a reputation as an author of epic poetry.

IXION: A murderous Thessalian king, who fathered the race of Centaurs upon a cloud he thought was the goddess Hera. His punishment in the Underworld was to be bound on a wheel and whipped with serpents.

JANUS GATE: A gate in Rome which was closed when there was peace, open when there was war.

JOVE: Another name for Jupiter, the head of the gods.

JUGURTHA: The Numidian ruler Jugurtha had been defeated by the Romans in the late second century B.C.E.

JUNO: The Roman Hera, Zeus's (Jupiter's) sister and wife.

JUPITER: The Roman name for Zeus, the head of the gods.

LACONIA: Sparta. Laconian dye was famous.

LAMIA: A friend of Horace's; member of a prominent family who traced their descent from Lamus, ancient king of Formiae, allegedly the town of the fabled Laestrygonians. Principal stress on the first syllable.

338

L A M U S : Ancient king of Formiae, south of Rome, alleged to be the town of the fabled Laestrygonians. The Lamia family claimed descent from Lamus.

L A P I T H S : *See* Centaurs and Lapiths.

L A R E S : Roman household gods.

L A R I S A : A region of Thessaly, in northern Greece.

L A T I U M : The region of Rome.

L A T O N A : The mother of Apollo and Diana, by Zeus.

L E D A : Mother of Castor and Pollux and of Helen of Troy.

L E S B O S : Sappho's native island; famous also for music and wine.

L E T H E : One of the five rivers of the Underworld.

L I B E R : Another name for Bacchus, the Liberator.

L I C E N T I A : Personification of sexual licentiousness.

L I C I N I U S : Lucius Licinius Murena. Brother-in-law, by adoption, of Maecenas. Executed in 23 B.C.E. after conspiring against Augustus.

L I R I S : A river in Latium.

L O L L I U S : Marcus Lollius, consul in 21 B.C.E.

L U C E R I A : An Apulian town well known for its wool.

L U C R E T I L I S : A hill near Horace's Sabine house. Principal stress on the second syllable.

L U C R I N U S , L A K E : A lake not far from Naples.

L U N A : Diana as Queen of the Moon.

L Y C I A : There was an oracle of Apollo at Patara, in Lycia, a region of Asia Minor.

L Y C U R G U S : King of Thrace, who suppressed the worship of Bacchus. In the blindness of his madness he killed his son, mistaking him for a tree, and cut off his own legs, mistaking them for branches.

L Y C Y M N I A : A pseudonym here for Maecenas's wife, Terentia.

L Y D I A N : Soft music associated with festivity.

M A E C E N A S : Horace's great friend and patron, Augustus's adviser and confidant. Horace had been welcomed into the circle of Maecenas by Virgil.

M A E N A D : A Bacchante, a female follower of Bacchus.

M A I A : The mother of Hermes (Mercury) by Zeus (Jupiter).

M A N L I U S : Manlius Torquatus, consul in 65 B.C.E.

M A R C E L L U S : Caesar's stepson and son-in-law, who died at an early age.

M A R I C A : A nymph, the wife of Faunus. There was a grove sacred to her at the mouth of the Liris River.

M A R S : The Roman god of war, son of Jupiter and Juno. His Greek name is Ares.

M A R S I A N S : An Italian tribe famous for its abilities in warfare.

M A R S I C W A R : The "Social War," between the Romans and other Italians, 90–89 B.C.E.

M A S S A G E T A E , G E T A E : A warlike people dwelling around the lower Danube.

M A S S I C : A fine Campanian wine.

M E D E S : A people related to the Parthians and dwelling near the Caspian Sea.

M E L P O M E N E : One of the Muses, of tragedy. But Horace often uses the names of the Muses in a more general sense.

M E M P H I S : Herodotus speaks of a temple to Aphrodite in this Egyptian city.

M E N E L A U S : King of Sparta; son of Atreus; brother of Agamemnon; husband of Helen.

M E R C U R Y : The trickiest god; god of travelers, including the dead going to Hades;

god of thieves, of language, of athletes, of commerce; inventor of the lyre. His mother was Maia, who was the daughter of Atlas.

M E R I O N E S : The charioteer of Idomeneus, king of Crete. Pronounced as a four-syllable word, stress on the first and fourth syllables.

M E T A U R U S : A river in Umbria, where Hasdrubal was defeated by the Romans.

M E T E L L U S : Consul in 60 B.C.E.

M I D A S : A Phrygian king, who asked that everything he touched be gold, and so it was—food, drink, and his daughter.

M I M A S : Giant who warred against the Olympian gods.

M I N E R V A : The Roman name for Athena, the goddess of wisdom.

M I N O S : King of Crete. In the *Odyssey*, XIX, 178, Homer speaks of him conversing with Zeus. After his death Minos was made a judge of the dead.

M I T Y L E N E : The hometown of Alcaeus and Sappho, on the island of Lesbos. It should be pronounced as a four-syllable word, stressed on the first and third syllables.

M Y C E N A E : An ancient city in the Peloponnesus. The city of Agamemnon.

N A I A D S : Water nymphs.

N E P T U N E : The Roman Poseidon, god of the sea.

N E R E I D S : Sea-maidens, attendants of Poseidon (Neptune).

N E R E U S : A sea-god. Principal stress on the first syllable.

N E R O : C. Claudius Nero helped defeat the Carthaginian leader Hasdrubal at the Metaurus River in Umbria. Drusus and Tiberius were descendants (and so, later on, was the emperor Nero).

N E S T O R : One of the greatest leaders against the Trojans, as an old man.

N I O B E : Niobe made fun of Latona, mother of Apollo and Diana, because Latona had only two children, while Niobe had many. As a result, almost all of Niobe's children were killed and Niobe was turned into stone.

N I P H A T E S : A mountain in Armenia.

N I R E U S : Homer called him the most beautiful of all the Greeks.

N O T U S : The South Wind from Africa, often causing storms on the Adriatic.

N U M I D I A : A desert region of Africa south of Carthage.

N Y M P H S : Divine maidens.

O L Y M P U S : The dwelling place of the gods, the highest Greek mountain, on the border between Thessaly and Macedonia.

O R C U S : Roman god of the Underworld.

O R I C U M : A town on the coast across the Adriatic from Brindisium.

O R I O N : A giant hunter, slain by Diana for attempting to rape her. He was turned into a constellation.

O R P H E U S : Son of Apollo and Calliope. Eurydice's husband. The great musician whose music almost succeeded in bringing Eurydice back to the world of the living.

P A L A T I N E : One of the Seven Hills of Rome, where there was a temple of Apollo.

P A L I N U R U S H E A D : A cape on the western coast of southern Italy. The context suggests that Horace was once in danger of drowning or shipwreck there.

P A N A E T I U S : A Greek philosopher of the second century B.C.E.

P A P H O S : A city on the island of Cyprus, with a shrine sacred to Aphrodite.

P A R I S : Seducer of Helen. One of the sons of Priam, king of Troy.

P A R R H A S I U S : A fifth-century B.C.E. Greek painter.

P A R T H I A N S : The Persians.

P A U L U S : M. Aemilius Paulus, who lost his life at the battle of Cannae, 216 B.C.E.

P A U L U S M A X I M U S : Paulus Fabius Maximus, consul in 11 B.C.E. He was a friend of Horace and also of Ovid and Augustus.

P E G A S U S : Bellerophon's wingèd horse.

P E L E U S : King of Thessaly, father of Achilles.

P E L I O N A N D O S S A : Mountains in Thessaly.

P E L O P S : Zeus's grandson; Tantalus's son; Atreus's father.

P E N A T E S : Roman household gods.

P E N E L O P E : Ulysses' faithful wife.

P E N T H E U S : King of Thebes, who failed to perceive that Bacchus (Dionysus) was a god. He was torn to pieces by the Bacchae.

P E R S E P H O N E : Her Latin name is Proserpina. Daughter of Demeter and Zeus. Ravished by Pluto and carried off to the Underworld to be his queen. She spends six months of the year as Queen of the Underworld.

P H A Ë T H O N : Apollo's son, who drove his father's chariot too near the sun.

P H I L I P O F M A C E D O N : The father of Alexander the Great.

P H I L I P P I : The scene of the battle in which Brutus and Cassius were defeated by Octavian (later Augustus), 42 B.C.E.

P H R A A T E S : He usurped the Parthian throne in 37 B.C.E., lost it, and then regained it.

P H R Y G I A : A region of Asia Minor.

P I E R I A : A place with a spring sacred to the Muses, near Mount Olympus.

P I N D A R : The sixth-century B.C.E. Greek poet.

P I N D U S : A mountain in Thessaly associated with the Muses.

P I R I T H O U S : King of the Lapiths. He tried to kidnap Proserpina and as punishment was chained forever in the Underworld.

P L A N C U S : L. Munatius Plancus, a Roman general and consul, whose home was at Tibur, in the region of Horace's Sabine farm.

P L E I A D E S : The daughters of Atlas became a constellation. In the fall they are associated with stormy weather.

P L U T O : The Latin name of Hades, the god of the Underworld.

P O L L I O : Gaius Asinius Pollio, consul, advocate, military commander, tragic poet, historian, founder of the first public library in Rome. He was a friend of Catullus, Virgil, and Horace. Virgil addressed him in the fourth Eclogue.

P O L L U X : One of the twin sons of Zeus (as a swan) and Leda, and brother of Helen. A great boxer. He and his brother Castor became the constellation Gemini, said to be able to bring calm to the waters.

P O L Y H Y M N I A : The Muse of sacred song.

P O M P I L I U S : Second king of Rome.

P O R P H Y R I O N : Giant who warred against the Olympian gods.

P O S T U M U S : Not certainly identified, though there have been various speculations.

P R A E N E S T E : A mountain town in Latium now called Palestrina.

P R I A M : King of Troy when Troy fell.

P R O C N E : When Tereus, the king of Thrace, assaulted Philomela, the sister of Procne, his wife, Philomela, and Procne took their revenge by killing Itylus, the child of Procne and Tereus, and serving him to Tereus for dinner. Philomela was turned into a nightingale, Tereus into a hoopoe, and Procne into a swallow.

P R O C U L E I U S : A high minister of Augustus, he shared his estate with his impoverished brothers.

P R O E T U S : See *Iliad*, VI, 178ff.

P R O M E T H E U S : In some stories, Prometheus is spoken of as creating human beings out of clay. He stole fire from heaven; brought civilization and disease down upon us; was punished, rescued by Hercules, and became a god.

P R O S E R P I N A : The Latin name of Persephone.

P R O T E U S : A sea-god.

P U N I C : Carthaginian.

P Y R R H A : The wife of Deucalion, "the Greek Noah." They restarted the human race, he by throwing stones which became men, she by throwing stones which became women. This Pyrrha, mentioned in i.2, has nothing to do with the young woman in i.5.

P Y T H A G O R A S : Mathematician and philosopher of the sixth century B.C.E. He encouraged belief in reincarnation.

P Y T H O : Delphi, on Mount Parnassus.

Q U I N C T I U S   H I R P I N U S : A friend of Horace's, not otherwise identified, although there have been various speculations. The context (ii.11) suggests he was a statesman of some sort.

Q U I N T I L I U S : Quintilius Varus, a friend of Horace and Virgil. Horace praises him as a judicious critic in the *Ars Poetica*.

Q U I R I N U S : The name of Romulus, founder of Rome, after he was deified; a name associated with his father, the god Mars.

R E G I A : The residence of the Pontifex Maximus in the Roman Forum.

R E G U L U S : Marcus Atilius Regulus, consul several times in the third century B.C.E. As commander in Africa he was defeated by Xanthippus. A captive of the Carthaginians sent back to Rome to negotiate an exchange of prisoners, Regulus refused to do so, so the story goes, for the reasons he states in the poem. He suffered the consequences foretold at the end of Ode iii.5.

R H A E T I A N   A L P S : The southern region of what are now called the Austrian Alps.

R H A E T I A N S : An Alpine tribe.

R H O D E S : A large island off the coast of Asia Minor.

R H O D O P E : A mountain in Thrace.

R H O E T U S : One of the Giants who warred against the Olympian gods.

R O M U L U S : Son of Mars and a mortal mother; brother of Remus, whom he killed. The founder of Rome, he became the god Quirinus.

S A B I N E : Horace's villa near Rome and still nearer Tibur (Tivoli) was in a region that had been inhabited by a tribe called the Sabines.

S A L A M I S : An island in the Aegean near Athens. Principal stress on the first syllable.

S A L I A N : The Salian priests of Mars danced a leaping dance. The name derives from *salire*, "to leap."

S A L L U S T I U S : Gaius Sallustius Crispus, a very rich man, descendant of the historian Sallust. He became Augustus's principal adviser.

S A P P H O : The great woman poet, seventh century B.C.E., who lived on the island of Lesbos.

S A T U R N : A Titan, the Roman Chronos, father of Jupiter, Juno, Neptune, Ceres. Jupiter usurped his throne.

S C A U R U S : M. Aemilius Scaurus, consul in 115 B.C.E.

S C I P I O : Scipio Africanus Major, conqueror of Hannibal at Zama in 202 B.C.E.; Scipio Aemilianus Africanus Numantinus conquered Carthage in 156 B.C.E.

S C O P A S : A fourth-century B.C.E. sculptor.

S C Y T H I A N S : A people who lived along the river Tanais, now called the Don, a river in what is now Russia. Expert riders and archers.

S E M E L E : Mother of Dionysus (Bacchus). Trisyllabic, principal stress on the first syllable. Zeus (Jupiter) was Bacchus's father.

S E R E S : The Chinese.

S E S T I U S : Lucius Sestius, consul in 23 B.C.E.

S I D R A : A bay off the coast of North Africa, and its desert island and shore. Sidra is the modern name.

S I M O N I D E S : A sixth-century B.C.E. Greek elegiac writer.

S I S Y P H U S : Condemned by Zeus, for various crimes, perpetually to roll a great stone uphill, which perpetually rolled back down.

S I T H O N I A N S : Thracians, with a reputation for drunkenness.

S O R A C T E , M O U N T : A mountain twenty miles north of Rome.

S P A R T A C U S : A gladiator who led a rebellion against Rome in 73–71 B.C.E.

S T E S I C H O R U S : A seventh-century B.C.E. poet who lived in Sicily.

S T H E N E L U S : Diomedes' charioteer in the Trojan War. Principal stress on the first syllable.

S T Y X : One of the five rivers of the Underworld.

S U L P I C I U S : There were storehouses by this name at the foot of the Aventine.

S Y G A M B R I A N S : A German tribe.

T A E N A R U S : A cape on the southern coast of the Peloponnesus; location of an entrance to the Underworld.

T A N A I S : The ancient name of the river Don, in Russia.

T A N T A L U S : Stole Zeus's dog; stole ambrosia and nectar from heaven; father of Pelops and thus father of the house of Atreus. Killed Pelops. His punishment in the Underworld was to be near food and water which perpetually eluded him.

T A R E N T U M : A city in Apulia near Horace's birthplace. Its modern name is Taranto.

T A R Q U I N : Tarquinius Superbus, the last king of Rome.

T E C M E S S A : A Trojan woman captured by the Greeks; Ajax's prize.

T E L A M O N : Father of Ajax.

T E M P E : A pleasant valley near Mount Olympus in Thessaly. Sacred to Apollo.

T E U C E R : A great archer in the Trojan War, half brother of Ajax. His father exiled him from Salamis because he had not avenged his brother's death.

T H E B E S : A Grecian city associated with Bacchus.

T H E S E U S : A legendary Grecian hero, slayer of the Minotaur. He helped Pirithous, king of the Lapiths, in his battle with the Centaurs.

T H E T I S : A sea-goddess, mother (by Peleus, king of Thessaly) of Achilles.

T H R A C E : The vast region which is now northeastern Greece and southern Bulgaria.

T H Y E S T E S : Brother of Atreus.

T I B U L L U S : Albius Tibullus, the elegiac poet, friend of Horace and of Virgil.

T I B U R : Now called Tivoli, a town near Horace's home.

T I G R I S : A river in Mesopotamia.

T I T A N S : Giant children of the ancient pre-Olympian gods.

T I T H O N U S : Priam's brother. The dawn fell in love with him and granted him immortality but not perpetual youth. Eventually he turned into a grass-hopper.

T I T Y O S : A giant killed by Apollo and Diana for insulting their mother. In the Underworld vultures fed on his ever-renewing liver.

T I V O L I : The modern name of Tibur, a town near Horace's Sabine villa.

T R O I L U S : A son of Priam, king of Troy; killed in the Trojan War.

T U L L U S : (1) An early king of Rome. (2) A consul in the year Horace was given his Sabine farm by Maecenas.

T U S C A N Y : A region of northwestern Italy along the Tyrrhenian Sea; inhabited by the Etruscans before Roman times.

T Y D E U S : Father of Diomedes.

T Y D I D E S : Diomedes. Principal stress on the second syllable.

T Y P H O E U S : One of the Giants who warred against the Olympian gods.

T Y R R H E N I A N   S E A : That part of the Mediterranean that washes the west coast of Italy.

U L Y S S E S : One of the great leaders of the Greeks against the Trojans; the hero of Homer's *Odyssey*, the story of his long voyage home after the Trojan War.

U S T I C A : A valley near Horace's Sabine house.

V A L G I U S : C. Valgius Rufus, a friend of Horace's, a translator and grammarian.

V A R I U S : Lucius Varius Rufus, a dramatist and writer of epic poetry, very much admired by both Virgil and Horace.

V A T I C A N   H I L L S : The hills on the other side of the Tiber, across from the Theater of Pompey.

V E N A F R U M : A town in Latium, near Rome, well known for its olive oil.

V E N U S : The Roman name of Aphrodite, goddess of love.

V E N U S I A : Horace's birthplace, in Apulia.

V E S T A : The goddess of hearth and home. Her temple was in the Forum.

V I A   S A C R A : The processional route through the Forum and up to the Capitol.

V I N D E L I C I : An Alpine tribe. Principal stress on the first syllable.

V I R G I L : The great poet Publius Vergilius Maro, who wrote the Eclogues, the Georgics, and the *Aeneid*. He was a close friend of Horace's and helped in-troduce him into the circle of Augustus and Maecenas.

V O L T O R E ,   M O U N T : An Apulian mountain near Horace's birthplace.

V U L C A N : The Roman name of Hephaestus, god of fire and of smithing.

X A N T H U S : A river in what is now Turkey. On its banks at Patara, there was a temple to Apollo.